Ben Franklin's
12 Rules
of Management

Blaine McCormick

Ben Franklin's 12 Rules of Management

Entrepreneur.
Press

Managing Editor: Marla Markman
Book Design: Sylvia H. Lee
Copy Editor: Ellen French
Proofreader: Tammy Ditmore
Cover Design: Mark A. Kozak
Interior and Cover Illustrations: Neil Shigley
Indexer: Ken DellaPenta

©2000 by Entrepreneur Media Inc.

This publication is designed to provide accurate and authoritative information in regard to the subject matter covered. It is sold with the understanding that the publisher is not engaged in rendering legal, accounting or other professional services. If legal advice or other expert assistance is required, the services of a competent professional person should be sought.

Library of Congress Cataloging-in-Publication Data
McCormick, Blaine.
Ben Franklin's 12 rules of management : the founding father of American business solves your toughest problems / by Blaine McCormick.
  p. cm.
Includes index.
ISBN 1-891984-14-4
1. Industrial management. 2. Franklin, Benjamin, 1706–1790
—Quotations. I. Title: Ben Franklin's twelve rules of management.
II. Title.
HD31 .M3827 2000
658—dc21   99-087362

Printed in Canada

09 08 07 06 05 04 03 02   10 9 8 7 6 5 4 3

*This book is dedicated to present and future members of
The Dead Managers Society.*

Acknowledgments

Every author is indebted to the influences that have shaped his thoughts and habits. As such, I would like to use a few paragraphs to acknowledge those individuals most responsible for this book.

First, I wish to thank Jere Yates of Pepperdine University for creating an environment that allowed nontraditional approaches to undergraduate business education. He offered his encouragement and support when I informed him that I wished to use *The Autobiography of Benjamin Franklin* and other literary classics as complementary texts in my undergraduate management class. The reading of great literature is on the decline in higher education and is virtually unheard of in business schools. This book was born out of those early experiments in the classrooms at Pepperdine University.

Second, I would like to thank those among my current colleagues at the Hankamer School of Business at Baylor University who provided me with much-needed counsel as I wrestled with the decision of whether to accept this project during the summer of 1999. They are Don Edwards, Duane Ireland, Linda Livingstone, Rick Martinez and J.T. Rose. Their comments helped immensely in shaping my commitment to writing this book. I would also like to thank Mike Robinson for stimulating my thinking on how to apply Franklin's concept of frugality to our modern business context.

Third, I would like to thank the people at Entrepreneur Media Inc. for their willingness to reshape company policy for the sake of this project. Specifically, I would like to thank my managing editor, Marla Markman, for wholeheartedly championing my interests during the negotiation process and for her great feedback and suggestions that immensely improved both the content and the flow of the text.

Fourth, I would like to thank my students who choose to tolerate a professor who makes them read more than they are accustomed to. Almost all the content of this book is a result of working with undergraduate business students for the past six years. These students are ultimately the heroes of both American society and of this book.

Fifth, I wish to thank those members of my church community who encouraged me and prayed for me during the writing of this book that God might bless me with the discipline and inspiration necessary to complete the task. They are David Beller, Blair Browning, Beth Dubis, Brent and Catherine Gibson, Greg Greer, Rob Holland, Tracy Sparks and Mark Wunnicke.

Lastly, I would like to thank my family for the richness they add to my life. A big thank you to my parents, Keith and Freida McCormick, for teaching me how to wake up early and do a task that I would rather avoid. A surprising amount of this book was written between 5 A.M. and 8 A.M. as a result of their influence. My wife, Sarah, proved to be a true companion. During the writing of this book, she was forced into assuming the unlikely roles of cheerleader, therapist and nurse—and she excelled at all three. Lastly, my thanks to our children, Ellis and Miriam, who have taught me more about management than even Benjamin Franklin could.

Table Of Contents

Introduction
The Founding Father
Of American Business xv

Chapter 1
Great Managers
Rarely Have Great Beginnings 1

Chapter 2
A Simple Recipe For Lifelong Learning 17

Chapter 3
How To Manage Others Effectively 33

Chapter 4
Winning In The End 47

Chapter 5
Hard Work And Frugality:
A Winning Combination 67

Chapter 6
Let Reason Work For You 85

Chapter 7
Becoming A Person Of Value 99

Chapter 8
Incentive Is Everything 119

Chapter 9
Doing The Impossible...................... 135

Chapter 10
Experiment! 147

Chapter 11
The Importance Of 1,001 Small Details ... 167

Chapter 12
A Good Reputation
Is Not An Accident 181

Conclusion
Becoming A Franklin-
Inspired Manager.......................... 195

Index 203

I now opened a little Stationer's Shop . . . [and] . . . began now gradually to pay off the Debt I was under for the Printinghouse.

—Benjamin Franklin,
quoted from his autobiography

Introduction

The Founding Father Of American Business

Before he became a patriot and Founding Father, Benjamin Franklin was a manager. This information may surprise people who have come to associate the bespectacled Franklin solely with the patriots who founded the United States of America. Franklin is, without a doubt, one of the great figures in American history. He is also one of the great figures in American *business* history.

My own education left me woefully ignorant of American business history. If anything, I was taught that "robber baron" capitalists were at the root of most of the trouble in American history. Similarly, the caption under Andrew Carnegie's picture in my high school history book read "philanthropist"—giving no hint to the extraordinary business talent that first made the money that was later given away. Cyrus McCormick was never mentioned as critical to the abolition of slavery even though his commercialization of the reaper diminished the need to have extra labor in the agriculture industry. In short, my history education either portrayed business in a negative light or ignored any connection to business success in depicting its worthy historical characters.

It's no surprise, then, that I never learned about Benjamin Franklin's rather amazing business story. For years, my two images of Benjamin Franklin were as "patriot and Founding Father" and "the guy with a kite." Only later, as a result of my own self-education efforts, did I learn that Franklin became a scientist and patriot because his success as a business manager allowed him to retire at age 42 and pursue other interests.

A Brief Overview Of Franklin's Life

Benjamin Franklin took time at the end of his life to write his autobiography for the benefit of his descendants and—to a certain de-

Will Power

t is said that your priorities become clearer the closer you get to death. If Franklin's last will and testament is any indication of his life's priorities, then our history books are in dire need of revision.

By anybody's standard, Franklin lived a remarkable life and assumed a wide variety of social roles and identities. This multitude of accomplishments is prioritized in the first line of his will: "I, Benjamin Franklin of Philadelphia, Printer, late Minister Plenipotentiary from the United States of America to the Court of France, now President of the State of Pennsylvania, do make and declare my last will and testament as follows: . . ."

Those first six words put it all into perspective, "I, Benjamin Franklin of Philadelphia, *Printer*. . . ." Near the end of his life Franklin gave due credit to the place his character was molded more than any other. In the obscurity of the printing house, he learned to manage himself and others. In the end, Franklin knew where he had his true beginning.

gree—himself. Readers of *The Autobiography of Benjamin Franklin* invariably find the text to be disjointed, grammatically unfamiliar and ultimately incomplete. In all fairness to Franklin, however, if you are willing to struggle with those shortcomings, you will also find it a witty and insightful <u>self-help</u> *tour de force*.

This book seeks to cull through Franklin's original text with an eye toward highlighting the principles that made him an effective individual and a successful small-business owner. Franklin's autobiography details only the first 51 years of his 84-year life. Most history scholars lament that Franklin stopped writing just as his life became the most interesting—as patriot, statesman and ambassador. Such a perspective, however, assumes that business has done little or nothing to mold the national character of America.

Franklin's autobiography is worthy of attention primarily because it accurately captures the years that shaped Franklin's character more than any other—his years as a printer and small-business owner. Although his life will be discussed in depth throughout this book, a brief overview here will help you more quickly grasp Franklin's rise from obscurity to greatness.

Franklin was born in Boston in 1706, the youngest son of Josiah Franklin, a soap and candle maker. Early in his life, Franklin demonstrated leadership qualities when playing with other children, as well as a love of reading. As a result of his literary interests, he was apprenticed into the printing trade at age 12 under his older brother James. Franklin found his brother's supervision undesirable, however, and left after a few years to work for a printer in Philadelphia.

Shortly thereafter, Franklin set up his own printing house in Philadelphia and met with great success. He married Deborah Read after establishing himself in business and then expanded his business interests by establishing silent partnerships with printing houses throughout the American colonies. In conjunction with these partnerships, Franklin ventured into the manufacture of ink and the paper supply business, and he served as creditor for some of his partners. When Franklin gave up active practice as a printer in 1748, he was regarded as the leader in the American printing trade. Given that printed matter was the dominant communication form in Colonial America, it's not too much of a stretch to say that Franklin might have been a media visionary on the scale of Ted Turner or Rupert Murdoch.

Following his retirement from printing, Franklin began to devote more of his time to public projects. He is credited with establishing Philadelphia's first public library, fire company, hospital, militia and night watch, and university. He expanded his influence into the international arena and represented Pennsylvania as its agent in England, resolving some taxation issues. Franklin's autobiography ends at this point.

Franklin continued his electricity experiments and in 1759 was awarded an honorary doctorate from the University of St. Andrews in Scotland. His successful appearances before the English court resulted in an appointment to several Colonial governorships before the beginning of the Revolutionary War. As taxation frustrations increased among the colonials and war loomed on the horizon, the British government turned more frequently to Franklin as a respected agent of compromise. Insulting personal attacks from the British, however, resulted in Franklin becoming an ardent Revolutionary and helping to finance the activities of the Continental Congress. Franklin served the war effort effectively as ambassador to France, procuring funding for the revolutionary effort from the court of Louis XVI .

Franklin returned to Philadelphia in 1785 and served as one of Pennsylvania's delegates to the Constitutional convention. He is credited with negotiating compromise among the warring state factions, which resulted in ratification of a single, all-encompassing constitution. Franklin spent the last two years of his life in great pain suffering from gout. His last public act was a position paper advocating the abolition of slavery. He died in 1790 at age 84.

Franklin's Business Legacy

Benjamin Franklin was not only one of the first great small- business managers in Colonial America, but also, in many respects, the archetype of the American businessperson. His life of public service and the subsequent popularity of his autobiography have left a unique and indelible stamp on the business activity of the following 200 years in America. In the early 1900s, the great German sociologist Max Weber wrote about Franklin in his well-known book, *The Protestant Work Ethic and the Spirit of Capitalism.* Weber chose none other than Benjamin Franklin to embody the capitalist ethic in its purest form. And so, it may not be too much of an exaggeration to refer to Franklin not only as a Founding Father but also as "the Founding Father of American Business."

Franklin's management legacy extends through more than one generation of American managers. One of his most notable devotees was the great steel entrepreneur Andrew Carnegie. Like Franklin, Carnegie rose from the obscurity of mundane jobs to almost mythical stature in American industrial history. Carnegie's admiration for Franklin is exhibited not only in his quoting Franklin in his own autobiography but also in his keeping contact with Franklin's descendants some three generations later. Carnegie also honored Franklin with some of his own philanthropic activities. When Franklin died, he left $5,000 to the city of Boston asking it to remain untouched and accumulate interest for 100 years. When the century was over, the original $5,000 investment had ballooned to $420,000, and Boston decided to use the funds to build the Franklin Institute— an evenings-only trade school designed to serve the educational

The Highly Effective Franklin

ne of the most influential business books of the late 20th century has been Stephen R. Covey's *The Seven Habits of Highly Effective People*. Since its publication in 1989, Covey's book has become required reading and recommended lifestyle at thousands of companies throughout America and the world. Covey endorses a philosophy of life he calls the "Character Ethic," which is based on the idea that human existence is governed by objective, fundamental principles that must be conformed to for maximum effectiveness in life. Covey points to Benjamin Franklin's autobiography as the embodiment of the Character Ethic. Covey lauds Franklin for living a life that attempted to integrate fundamental principles into daily habits and routines. Although Covey was not the first to recognize Franklin's influence in his own life, he is certainly one of the most prominent and credible individuals to do so in recent times.

needs of tradesmen wanting to improve themselves. Unfortunately, the $420,000 was adequate only to construct buildings and purchase equipment, leaving the school without an endowment for operational expenses. Carnegie got word of the situation and provided $420,000 in matching funds for an operating endowment to honor his hero and support any future Franklins the school might produce. The school exists today as the Franklin Institute of Boston and offers a wide variety of technical degrees.

The financier Thomas Mellon also numbered himself among Franklin's admirers but even more so than Andrew Carnegie. Mellon states that reading Franklin's autobiography was the turning point in his life: It inspired him to leave a life of farming and produce one of this country's greatest fortunes. Later in his life, Mellon paid tribute to Franklin by printing 1,000 copies of Franklin's autobiography to give to the legions of young people who solicited Mellon's advice on business management. Furthermore, contrary to the established practice of the day, Mellon erected a statue of Franklin in his bank rather than decorate the lobby with a statue of himself.

Franklin's business legacy is not limited to fellow Pennsylvanians like Carnegie and Mellon who were born in the 1800s. Franklin's influence can also be found in one of the great business success stories of the late 20th century: Berkshire Hathaway Inc. Berkshire Hathaway—better known as Warren Buffet's company—is a holding company in Omaha, Nebraska, with a variety of business interests ranging from insurance to candies to fast food. The company's investments are directed by Warren Buffet and his lesser-known silent partner, vice chairman Charles Munger. Munger stated in a 1996 interview with *Forbes* that his hero is none other than Benjamin Franklin, and both he and Buffet share an awesome respect for the idea of compounding interest popularized by Franklin. Roger Lowenstein, in his book on Warren Buffet, discusses Munger at length, stating that Munger finds Franklin's aphorisms more useful than what is taught in most business schools.

Munger told *Forbes* that he was leaving more and more of the investing to Buffet as he diverted his attention to nonbusiness-related projects. Where did Munger get the inspiration for such a move? He states he was trying to model his life after Benjamin Franklin, who left his business pursuits in midlife to work on projects with a broader impact.

America On The Rise

The 1990s have been a great decade for American management. When I went through business school in the 1980s, American management seemed to be breaking down, and professors pointed their students East toward the rising sun of Japanese-style management. Our Japanese associates taught us, among other things, that quality mattered and that there might be other ways to structure the employment relationship. When the stock market crashed in October 1987, pundits argued that American management had collapsed on itself and that our only hope lay in reinventing American management. Fast forward 13 years. . . .

The United States of America closes the 20th century as the most vibrant economy on the planet. We did indeed learn from the Japanese, and our quality improved and is still improving. However, no amount of quality advocacy can explain the revival and continued strength of the American economy. I believe the roots of America's current business success lie in the principles embodied more than 200 years ago in the life of the Founding Father of American Business, Benjamin Franklin. Franklin's life exemplifies the innovation, technology and ingenuity that have propelled the American economy to unprecedented heights in recent years. I know it sounds odd, but I see his footprint in almost every Silicon Valley success story I read.

The Design Of This Book

The material for this book is taken primarily from Franklin's autobiography. Any attempt to summarize and categorize his life, however, would be incomplete as it contains entirely too many lessons in too many divergent fields to capture in a single paperback. I make no pretense of completely emptying the autobiography of all its managerial lessons, for it is simply too rich a source. The core, however, of Franklin's management style is captured in these pages. And, I challenge each reader to meet Franklin one-on-one in the full text of his autobiography to gather the lessons that I have not mentioned or noticed.

This book is written for current and future corporate managers, supervisors and small-business owners. Good management is a skill that you can learn and implement daily to improve your own performance, the performance of your staff and workers, and ultimately the performance of your business. To help you put the messages of this book into practice, I've organized each chapter around one of Benjamin Franklin's 12 management rules.

Each chapter also includes quotes—"Benjamin Franklin Once Said . . ."—which include a short business-related commentary. One of Franklin's best-known legacies are the many clever and memorable sayings from his personal writings and almanacs. Even today, many people are surprised to discover that "God helps them that help themselves" is from Franklin's *Poor Richard's Almanac* and not the Bible. Franklin later referred to these sayings as "the wisdom of many ages and nations." Not all of them are 100 percent original; Franklin was well-read, and he drew from many sources for inspiration. Nonetheless, almost all these sayings have been filtered through Franklin's original mind and distilled with the wit, charm and brevity that distinguish his writing.

Finally, each chapter closes with a checklist of activities—"What Good Shall I Do This Day?"—which summarizes the basic lessons and challenges you to implement them daily. I wish I could take credit for this idea, but I can't. Challenging himself to seize each day as an opportunity to improve, Benjamin Franklin asked himself this question each morning when he arose. To remain true to the spirit of the man, I should offer no less in a book sharing his management philosophy and techniques with a broader audience.

A Book About Business, Not Leadership

This is not a book about leadership. Rather, it is about business. Specifically, it is about American business management. Leadership is necessary for a wide variety of social undertakings, from waging war to governing countries and undertaking movements to restore civil rights. Business, however, is always an economic undertaking, and making money involves very different principles from waging war.

Benjamin Franklin is certainly considered one of America's most influential leaders. His leadership role during Revolutionary America has

---

Franklin's 12 Rules Of Management

1. Finish better than your beginnings.
2. All education is self-education.
3. Seek first to manage yourself, then to manage others.
4. Influence is more important than victory.
5. Work hard and watch your costs.
6. Everybody wants to appear reasonable.
7. Create your own set of values to guide your actions.
8. Incentive is everything.
9. Create solutions for seemingly impossible problems.
10. Become a revolutionary for experimentation and change.
11. Sometimes it's better to do 1,001 small things right than only one large thing right.
12. Deliberately cultivate your reputation and legacy.

---

been briefly chronicled by Donald Phillips in *The Founding Fathers on Leadership*. (Phillips has written also on the leadership styles of Abraham Lincoln and Martin Luther King, Jr.) Other leadership books go as far as drawing leadership lessons from Jesus, Attila the Hun, Sitting Bull, Winston Churchill and even the fictional characters from "Star Trek." Every leader has a beginning, however, and Franklin's life of leadership began during his years as a businessman. Those years and those skills are the primary focus of this book. Although few are called to be leaders, everyone can learn to be a better manager.

Two Final Disclaimers

First, this book includes numerous and sometimes lengthy passages taken directly from *The Autobiography of Benjamin Franklin*. These quotations are included to show Franklin's original text and allow readers to savor the wit and wisdom that infuses his entire autobiography. The English Franklin used might seem a bit perplexing since he was born almost 300 years ago, but only seldom did he use such an obscure word that it is meaningless in the modern context.

However, you will find that Franklin often used some of the most peculiar grammar in contrast to current standards. In these passages, you will discover that nouns and verbs are often capitalized for no apparent reason. (Franklin had his reasons, but they do not need to be explained in a book about his management principles and techniques.)

Second, you will notice that Franklin liberally used the ampersand (*&*) and abbreviated his past tense verbs as *present'd* (for *presented*). I have left his abbreviations in the quotations to preserve the original flavor of Franklin's text. This shorthand is easier to explain than the grammar: Franklin wrote the entire autobiography by hand. And because time was money to Franklin, these simple abbreviations are evidence that he genuinely believed that the time saved by using "&" in place of "and" or "'d" instead of "—ed" could be redirected into more beneficial activities. If you think this last statement is an exaggeration, then suspend your disbelief for now and see if you draw the same conclusion at the end of the book.

I was dirty from my Journey; my Pockets were stuff'd out with Shirts & Stockings; I knew no Soul, nor where to look for Lodging. I was fatigued from Travelling, Rowing, & Want of Rest. I was very hungry, and my whole Stock of Cash consisted of a Dutch Dollar and about a Shilling of Copper.

—Benjamin Franklin
upon his arrival in Philadelphia

Chapter 1

Great Managers Rarely Have Great Beginnings

You've dreamed for years about starting your own business. You're ready to say goodbye to that day job at the supermarket and enjoy the freedom, excitement and financial rewards of being your own boss. You've even decided to put a few things on paper and rough out a business plan. Today's the day you've decided to sit down and determine exactly what's necessary to take your first step. "Let's see," you say to yourself, "what stands in the way of me and my own business?"

The first thing that comes to mind is a bit intimidating, but you write it down anyway: You need to finish college. You left college after your freshman year because it just didn't interest you. Now you're regretting it. Also, everything you read suggests that simply a college degree won't be enough. You need an MBA, too. All in all, you've got maybe five or six years of school staring you in the face.

Next, you start thinking about the office space you'll need to buy . . .

or, OK, rent. You sketch out an office for yourself, a front room for receiving clients, and an office for your secretary. Then there's the new office furniture, computer and phone equipment, and a great sign for the front.

You turn the page and start listing some personal things that you'll need before all this can become a reality. The list includes a reliable car that won't get you laughed at when you pick up a client and a business wardrobe to replace the casual dress you wear in the supermarket. You even start thinking about joining that expensive downtown health club to help build your network.

You lay down your pad and pencil in near frustration. "This is impossible!" you think to yourself. "Any hope I had for going into business ended when I left college. I'm finished. . . ." At this point, you're in dire need of Franklin's first management principle.

Franklin's First Rule Of Management:
Finish better than your beginnings.

Excuses, Excuses

We've all heard the legend that Franklin rose from obscurity to greatness, but few of us really understand just how obscure and downright miserable Franklin's early life was. Franklin's beginnings were so pathetic that he could have easily chosen to remain undistinguished. Faced with the same circumstances, many individuals would marshal a variety of excuses to explain their poor performance on the job or lack of success in life. Here's a brief list of Franklin's potential grievances.

● **Excuse 1: The youngest son.** Franklin was the youngest son of the youngest son for five generations. In the economic order of the day, the eldest child was usually given control of the family's assets upon the death of the father. The youngest son of the youngest son had little or no assets with which to navigate life.

Further, Franklin notes that it was custom in his family for the eldest son to be trained as a smith—or metalworker. Beyond this, it seems as though the remaining children were left without a plan. In fact, Franklin's own father was at such a loss regarding what to do with young Benjamin that he considered giving him as his tithe to his church. (*Tithe* is an old English word that is translated today as *one-tenth*.) It was common practice in the Puritan faith to give one-tenth of your income or worldly goods to the church. Josiah Franklin had 10 sons; therefore, he considered giving the youngest, Benjamin, as an offering to the church.

Benjamin Franklin had one thing going for him, however. He had been born in America. For the first time in human history, birth order would not determine an individual's destiny in Colonial America. America was established as a country where all able, motivated individuals could have the opportunity to become something better than what their birth order in a landed aristocracy would have allowed. America would become the first country where the nation's fortunes would not stay in the hands of a few families. Rather, new wealth could be created by almost anyone in almost any place. In his autobiography, Benjamin Franklin literally wrote the book about the self-made American success story.

- **Excuse 2: Beaten as an indentured servant.** A second excuse Franklin could have mustered in self-defense was that he began his working life as little more than a slave. Specifically, he was known as an indentured servant. Franklin writes,

> "In 1717 my Brother James return'd from England with a Press & Letters to set up his Business in Boston. I lik'd it much better than that of my Father, but still had a Hankering for the Sea. To prevent the apprehended Effect of such an Inclination, my Father was impatient to have me bound to my Brother. I stood out sometime, but at last was persuaded and signed the Indentures, when I was yet but 12 Years old. I was to serve as an Apprentice till I was 21 Years of Age. . . ."

Franklin's father was afraid his youngest son would run off to sea, which was the Colonial equivalent of running off to join the circus. Therefore, he apparently pressured young Benjamin to become an apprentice to his brother in the printing trade. Once he signed the papers of indenture, Franklin was bound to his brother for almost a decade. The formal name for this relationship was apprentice and master, but in reality the relationship was more like slave and master. The master provided room and board for the apprentice in exchange for the services of the apprentice in running the master's trade. Franklin noted later in his autobiography that he and his brother had numerous and increasingly frequent disputes. Furthermore, the brother disciplined Franklin by beating him.

A few years into his apprenticeship, Franklin seized the opportunity presented by a contractual redesign of his articles of indenture to escape from his brother's oversight. Franklin later felt some remorse for escaping on what was a cross between a legal technicality and a private deal between him and his brother. Nevertheless, the seeds of revolution were planted during Franklin's years as an indentured servant. Fortunately for his fellow citizens, those beatings gave Franklin a lifelong sensitivity to arbitrary power and the use of force to resolve conflicts.

Benjamin Franklin Once Said ...

"God helps them that help themselves."

Franklin's curious mix of a strong faith in God, the guiding hand of Providence, and a strong faith in self gave him a remarkable bias for action. Franklin argued that if a person believed in God but took no action on his or her own, then that person's life was not worthy of attention. He was often frustrated by Colonial religious groups who claimed that God would protect them from hostile attacks but did nothing to shore up their own defenses.

Although Franklin had a bias for action, he also believed that such action should be within certain limits. He took great care to conform his activities to what he believed to be moral laws that governed the universe. He never believed that a moral law granted unproductive individuals great rewards. He firmly believed that we must take the first steps. Our problems will not solve themselves, and, chances are, no one is coming to rescue us. Franklin didn't wait around for good things to happen. Rather, he discovered that rewards tend to follow well-directed action.

- **Excuse 3: No formal education.** Franklin's education is the focus of the next chapter. So for now, suffice it to say that Franklin was denied many educational resources that we take for granted today. Franklin had only a rudimentary grammar-school education and nothing that comes close to a modern college experience. In fact, Franklin's father deliberately curtailed his education for fear that Franklin would want to continue on to college, an expense his father was either unable or unwilling to support. However, as you will see in the next chapter, Franklin did not let the lack of a formal education impede his forward momentum.

The Surprising Origin Of Other Great American Businesspeople

If you've ever had a vision for your life and then thrown up your hands in frustration, this chapter's for you. Our fictional worker in the opening example has one thing going for him: He wants to improve his life. Franklin had the same desire, and he managed to rise from total obscurity to world acclaim by the end of his life. However, our fictional worker has placed an obstacle in his way that Franklin never did. Franklin finished better than his beginnings, and he demonstrated that you don't have to have a great beginning to have a great finish. Too many people try to construct impossible starting scenarios for entry into a personal business. In doing so, they defeat themselves before they ever get started. This chapter will show that some really great businesses have been started in garages (and worse) and by college dropouts (and worse). The difference is that they just decided to start where they were. Let's take a look at the beginnings of five legendary businesspeople (and one soon-to-be legend) that span the two centuries between Franklin's time and ours.

- **John D. Rockefeller of the Standard Oil Company:** The founder of the greatest fortune ever earned on American soil came from surprisingly modest beginnings. John D. Rockefeller was born in rural western New York in 1839. His parents provided a solid home for the Rockefeller children, of which John was the eldest son. His father worked as a farmer and then engaged in a variety of business interests. Although the family made a comfortable living, they certainly were not considered wealthy.

Rockefeller demonstrated an aptitude for business at a young age. One of his earliest ventures was raising turkeys, then lending the money he accumulated and collecting interest on the accounts. Throughout these early dealings, John D. demonstrated remarkable frugality, hard work and keen foresight.

After graduating from high school in 1855, Rockefeller earnestly sought and gained employment as a bookkeeper and clerk in a Cleveland merchant house. The experience provided him with a strong business foundation. Also, from his earliest days in business, Rockefeller kept track of his financial dealings—revenues, interest and church tithes—in a small book he called Ledger A. From these simple rural beginnings, Rockefeller went on to build the first great modern corporation, the Standard Oil Company.

- **Andrew Carnegie of the Carnegie Steel Co.:** Unlike both Franklin and Rockefeller, Andrew Carnegie was not born in America. As such, he became one of the greatest immigrant success stories in American history. Carnegie was born in Dunfermline, Scotland, in 1835, the son of a handloom weaver. The introduction of power looms into Scotland forced the family to relocate, and they chose to go across the Atlantic to America. Ultimately the family settled in what is now Pittsburgh, Pennsylvania.

Young Andrew soon found work in a cotton factory, while his father continued to sell his product door to door. Later Carnegie took a job as an office clerk and began attending night classes to learn double-entry bookkeeping. His next job was as a messenger boy for a Pittsburgh telegraph office.

Carnegie used the telegraph job as the springboard to his future success. Mainly through self-discipline and self-education, he rose from messenger boy to telegraph operator and later was a telegraph operator for the Pennsylvania Railroad, the largest and most complex organization of the day. From this point, Carnegie made investments and began building interests in the emerging American steel industry. He went on to become its most dominant figure.

- **Walt Disney of the Walt Disney Co.:** The man most responsible for much of our modern entertainment industry got off to a less than stellar start. Walter Elias Disney was born in Chicago in 1901, but his family quickly moved to a rural farming area. Walt Disney was the fourth son of Elias Disney, an always eager-to-move jack-cfall-trades, and Flora Call, a schoolteacher. His restless father later moved the family to Kansas City and tried earning a living delivering newspapers with his sons.

While in Kansas City, the young Walt learned important lessons in self-discipline from delivering newspapers, rain or shine. He began taking classes at the Kansas City Art Institute and School of Design. Disney eventually landed a job as a newspaper cartoonist, but World War I interrupted his career for a few years.

After returning from the war, Disney produced his first cartoons but was cheated out of them by a crafty film distributor from New York. Down but not out, Disney traveled west to Los Angeles and continued making short animated films in the newly christened film capital. In 1928, Disney and his associates produced a short cartoon with sound starring a cheerful fellow named Mickey Mouse, who had appeared in two earlier "silent" cartoons. The film, "Steamboat Willie," was a sensation, and Disney was on his way. His obscure beginnings and early failures gave few hints of the entertainment greatness of Disney's legacy. In particular, he would leave an indelible mark on full-length animated films, amusement parks and early television.

● **Mary Kay Ash of Mary Kay Cosmetics:** Mary Kay's rags-to-riches story rivals Franklin's in its drama and social significance. Mary Kay's story begins when she got married right out of high school because she couldn't afford college. Her husband was drafted for World War II and left her at home with young children. The military pay wasn't enough to make ends meet, so Mary Kay took a job with Stanley Home Products selling household specialties at home parties. In this job she learned that she had a natural sense for selling.

She remained with Stanley for well over a decade but suffered through a divorce and was left to provide for three children. Ash then moved to Dallas and began work as national training director for World Gifts. After 20 years in corporate America, she concluded that it was a man's world designed for the enjoyment and advancement of men rather than women.

After Mary Kay remarried, she and her second husband decided to begin their own company, one they hoped would be more female-friendly. Unfortunately, he died a month before they could launch it. This divorced, widowed, undercapitalized and under-appreciated grandmother decided to go forward anyway. With the help of her 20-year-old son, Richard, and $5,000 in capital, she launched Mary Kay Cosmetics and began a revolution that changed the role of women in corporate America.

- **Andrew Grove of Intel:** *Time* magazine's 1997 Man of the Year was born Andras Grof in Budapest, Hungary, in 1936, the son of a Jewish dairyman. When the German tanks rolled into Hungary, he and his family had to go into hiding and remain there for the duration of the war. The end of the war brought little relief to most of the country, and things took a turn for the worse in 1956 when the Soviet Army invaded and established Communist rule.

  Following the Soviet invasion, Grove escaped from Hungary and departed for America on a rusty ship designed to transport American troops during the war. His arrival in America was anticlimactic, but he did receive a much-needed hearing aid from the International Rescue Committee, and hearing lost in a childhood illness was restored. Barely able to speak English, Grove obtained a job as a waiter and enrolled in classes at the City College of New York.

  Despite his initial difficulties, Grove went on to graduate at the top of his chemical engineering class in 1960. He continued his education at the University of California, Berkeley, and received a Ph.D. in chemical engineering in 1963. Following graduation, he took a job at Fairchild Semiconductor in research and development while continuing to teach at UC Berkeley.

  In 1968, Bob Noyce and Gordon Moore started a company called Intel, and Grove was one of their first two employees. Grove went on to become the firm's third CEO, following Intel's two founders in the role. In many ways, Grove's management shepherded Intel through what he later called the "Valley of the Shadow of Death," referring to the world's transition from mainframe computers to personal computers. Despite the turbulent environment, Intel ultimately emerged as one of the dominant firms of the Digital Age.

- **Michael Dell of Dell Computer:** The soon-to-be-legendary Michael Dell started his now-famous computer company in a dorm room at the University of Texas, Austin. As an 18-year-old freshman, Dell began building and upgrading the capabilities of personal computers. When the business boomed, he stopped pretending to be a pre-med major and dropped out of school to continue building his company. Central to Dell's success has been his ability to skirt traditional middlemen in retail environments.

Dell grew up in Houston, the son of an orthodontist and a stockbroker. He showed business acumen early in his life. At 13, he made

Why I Love Trash

ne of my personal mottos is, "Give me the trash. I can always make it look better!" I'm glad to be handed the least popular and most boring class in the college catalog, because, chances are, I'm not going to make it any worse. More likely, I'm going to set my sights on turning it into a wonderful course that everybody wants to take. I've found that it's easy to make improvements on what others believe is trash.

One company that's taken trash and turned it into gold is ServiceMaster. In 1929, Marion Wade founded ServiceMaster as a moth-proofing company in the Chicago area. The company flourished and expanded into the carpet-cleaning business in 1952. A decade later, they pioneered outsourcing by contracting for some of the regular maintenance work in the health-care industry. Over the years, the company has created ways of taking on more and more of the regular maintenance and cleaning jobs of other businesses. The firm is now the national leader for outsourcing in facilities management.

When you take a close look at ServiceMaster's portfolio of services, you will be immediately struck by how mundane the businesses seem. Lawn care, landscaping, residential and commercial cleaning, pest control, plumbing and drain cleaning, and air vent cleaning are nobody's idea of glamorous businesses. Yet ServiceMaster took what others considered "trashy" work and turned it into a successful, branded international business. Furthermore, their strong commitment to developing their employees has helped them attract above-average talent in a labor market notorious for low-quality workers. Next time you are looking for a new market niche, you may find great opportunity in the most unattractive places.

$2,000 trading stamps on consignment using a rented mailbox. Rather than trade through somebody else's auctions, Dell and a friend set up their own auction and made more money by cutting out the middleman—a lesson that was foundational to the Dell Computer company less than a decade later.

As a teenager, Dell learned the benefits of targeting customer segments rather than use more shotgun-style approaches to marketing. He would get a list of marriage license applicants once a week from the Houston courthouse and send personalized letters produced on his Apple IIe inquiring about their interest in subscribing to the *Houston Post*. He experienced better success than his competitors with this targeted approach, and another seed was planted for the future.

Dell learned his first computer industry lessons by visiting computer retailers. He noticed that when a computer was sold, the retailer kept a sizable chunk of the selling price and sent the rest to the manufacturer. The young Dell surmised that the retailer wasn't adding any value to the sale, especially for sophisticated consumers, and the seed of another idea was planted.

When he started his own computer business, Dell sold the hardware using a direct model almost out of necessity. He serviced rather sophisticated customers he reached through ads in specialized trade magazines. Contact with almost all customers was by telephone. They likely would not have been overly impressed to visit his dormitory-based manufacturing facility.

Dell's direct marketing model and PC business revolutionized the computer industry. He currently ranks in the top 10 richest Americans, according to *Forbes*. He began with almost no capital and no real strategy other than technological opportunism—not bad for a college dropout. Then again, Benjamin Franklin never had the benefit of college, either.

Prisons Of Our Own Making

It's a commonly believed myth in America that you have to be born great to achieve greatness. Franklin's life and the life of other managers chronicled in this chapter shatter that myth. A myth is ultimately a lie, and a lie is a prison from which we can escape. Franklin's life clearly demonstrates his escape from four kinds of prisons: birth, circumstance, ignorance and error. Let's discuss them in detail and show exactly how Franklin liberated himself.

● **The prison of birth:** Franklin was born a rather ordinary child to rather ordinary parents in a rather ordinary house near a rather ordinary city. There was no inherited wealth that his father, Josiah Franklin, could draw upon to ensure a good life for his children. Further, Franklin was an ocean removed from the most extraordinary places of his day, London and Paris.

Few of us reading this book came into the world with everything we needed to achieve the success we desire. Say hello to a guy who understands: Benjamin Franklin. Rather than stay in the prison of birth, Franklin decided to free himself, and the key he used was hard work. Primarily through hard work and creation of wealth, Franklin achieved a measure of success in his life that could not have been predicted by his humble beginnings. Hard work was the key that unlocked the prison of birth.

● **The prison of circumstance:** We all do time in the prison of circumstance. From time to time, circumstances seem to get the best of us and we find ourselves in situations—sometimes of our own making—which seem virtually impossible to get out of. Franklin found himself the prisoner of circumstance on several occasions: when he was indentured to his rather abusive older brother and when he fell into the company of loose women as a lusty youth. Fortunately, he was able to free himself with the key of mobility.

When Franklin found a situation too hard to bear, he simply got up and left. It may sound too obvious and somewhat irresponsible, but it produced some remarkable outcomes. When Franklin could no longer bear his brother's beatings, he ran away. When he could no longer resist the temptation of loose women, he ran away. Whenever possible, Franklin later did what he could to make the matter right. For example, he cared for his abusive brother's child when his brother died unexpectedly, and he took as his own son an illegitimate child he fathered during a brief love tryst. Mobility was the key that unlocked the prison of circumstance.

● **The prison of ignorance:** Everybody begins life in the prison of ignorance. We don't know how to speak or walk or dress ourselves. As we grow older, we learn that we don't know how to read or solve algebraic equations or balance a checkbook. Franklin began life in this prison and often found himself locked back inside when he thought he had escaped. His path out of ignorance was through education.

When Franklin needed to expand his knowledge base, he bought or borrowed books. When he needed to learn more about the printing industry, he went to London for a few years to study the art in one of its most important cities. We too can use education to unlock the prison of ignorance. A common temptation is to pretend we aren't ignorant and try to fake our way through. Franklin's humility motivated him to quickly admit his shortcomings and seek to correct them.

● **The prison of error:** Hard-working, mobile and educated people often find themselves trapped in one last prison: the prison of error. We find ourselves in the prison of error when our knowledge becomes obsolete, when our world changes dramatically, and when

Benjamin Franklin Once Said ...

"In success be moderate."

If you commit yourself to finishing better than you began, you're more likely to succeed. When you begin making a great deal of money, Franklin would advise you to stay quiet about it. Don't rush out and build a more lavish office building or start driving flashy cars and throwing fancy parties. Worse yet, avoid talking up your new-found success in TV or print interviews. Visible success attracts two kinds of problems: imitation and regulation. You should avoid both as long as possible, but especially the latter.

I know a businessman who was hounded by regulatory agencies for more than six years even though he never broke a law. He confessed to me that he had brought the trouble on himself by being too visible about his success, bragging about it, and attracting the attention of regulators who were suspicious about his profits. The company was cleared of all charges in a court of law, but the businessman admitted that his trouble could have been easily avoided if he had been more moderate about his success.

our political opinions become outdated. Businesspeople most frequently find themselves in the prison of error when they attempt to build their business on the cutting edge where no prior knowledge or experience can guide decisions.

Experimentation is the key to escaping the prison of error. During Franklin's lifetime, there was a great deal of misinformation about the nature of lightning. In fact, a great majority of people believed that lightening could be explained only with mythology, and anyone who wished to tame it was nothing less than a magician. Franklin was not a magician but rather a genuine scientific leader when he first harnessed the destructive power of lightening. To uncover its physical laws, he conducted a variety of experiments, including his legendary kite-flying experiment. These experiments resulted in the invention of the lightning rod and saved many buildings from fire. Likewise, when Franklin was faced with new kinds of moral teachings, he would often experiment with some of the teachings to determine whether or not they actually led to more virtuous behavior and a better quality of life. For Franklin, the key of experimentation unlocked the prison of error.

Three Mistakes Franklin Never Made

Along with the many good decisions in his early years, Franklin also avoided making some mistakes that would have stalled the progress of otherwise capable people. Avoiding these mistakes helped keep Franklin on the road to personal and business effectiveness.

● **Accepting the status quo:** One of my favorite films is "Lawrence of Arabia." I love it when Lawrence risks his life to rescue a colleague by crossing the hottest part of the desert in the middle of the day. His friends tell him that he's crazy to go back into the desert because "it is written" that nobody can survive the heat. Lawrence succeeds in the rescue, of course, and triumphantly declares to his friends upon his return that, "Nothing is written!"

Franklin had the same attitude in many respects. He never believed that he had to be the least in the family just because he was the youngest son. He never accepted that beatings were just a part of being an apprentice that had to be tolerated. Put simply, he never accepted the status quo but rather used it as a benchmark to check his progress.

- **Waiting for something good to happen:** Franklin's early circumstances were so devoid of opportunity that he was forced to go elsewhere to seek his fortune, and he did go elsewhere. Too many people wait around hoping that opportunity somehow will come their direction. These same people sit and complain that all the good things happen to other "lucky" people. In fact, I've met a number of people who make the astounding claim of being "unlucky"— as if life or fate or whatever had singled them out for a special brand of persecution.

- **Waiting for the generosity of others:** Franklin did not align his fortunes with the favors that other people might or might not throw his way. I know people who are depending on their wealthy parents to either voluntarily share their money or die and leave them a significant inheritance. I know others who depend on political favors from elected officials to improve their business prospects. Franklin was willing to accept help from influential people, but he never made it the crux of his action plan. When generosity did appear, he gratefully accepted it. When it did not, he continued to pursue his own agenda.

The greatest compliment I can give Benjamin Franklin is that he became something that no social scientist could have predicted. Social scientists are fond of predicting a person's career and income level based on demographic data. Franklin would have turned those prediction models upside down! He continued to become something that was more than a product of his environment. And in doing so, he taught us that we can all finish better than we begin.

What Good Shall I Do This Day?

❑ Never let your beginnings be an excuse for failing to improve yourself.

❑ Start where you are today improving yourself rather than always wishing things were better.

❑ Avoid the temptation to do every improvement at once. Rather, improve yourself one small step at a time.

❑ Unlock the prison of birth with the key of hard work.

❑ Unlock the prison of circumstance with the key of mobility.

❑ Unlock the prison of ignorance with the key of education.

❑ Unlock the prison of error with the key of experimentation.

❑ Don't accept the status quo as your destiny. "Nothing is written!"

❑ Don't wait for something good to happen to you. Rather, make something good happen.

❑ Don't let your future depend on the generosity of others.

❑ If somebody hands you trash, view it as an opportunity for easy improvement.

From a Child I was fond of Reading, and all the little Money that came into my Hands was ever laid out in Books. Pleas'd with the Pilgrim's Progress, my first Collection was of John Bunyan's Works, in separate little Volumes. I afterwards sold them to enable me to buy R. Burton's Historical Collections; they were small Chapmen's Books and cheap, 40 or 50 in all. My Father's little Library consisted chiefly of books in polemic Divinity, most of which I read, and have since often regretted, that at a time when I had such a Thirst for Knowledge, more proper Books had not fallen in my Way, since it was now resolv'd I should not be a Clergyman. Plutarch's Lives there was, in which I read abundantly, and I still think that time spent to great Advantage. There was also a Book of Defoe's, called an Essay on Projects, and another of Dr. Mather's, call'd Essays to Do Good which perhaps gave me a Turn of Thinking that had an Influence on some of the principal future Events of my Life.

—Benjamin Franklin
discussing his personal reading habits

Chapter 2

A Simple Recipe For Lifelong Learning

"**C**ongratulations, you're obsolete!"
Each semester I share with my students the simple but depressing message that much of their skill base will be obsolete by the time they graduate from college. Many of them express anger that they are paying thousands of dollars in tuition money just to be officially certified as obsolete upon graduation. I console them by letting them know that it's a privilege to be officially certified as obsolete by an American university. Further, this certification of official obsolescence will still significantly raise their salaries and provide them with greater job opportunities than those without it.

All this talk about skill obsolescence opens the door for a discussion about keeping current in our modern society. Much of the content in traditional college business textbooks is at best one to two years behind market knowledge. How, then, can students close the gap between old knowledge and current knowledge? Here is the good news. I tell them that if we've done our job right as professors, then most of the self-education skills necessary to close the knowledge gap have already been instilled in them. Overcoming obsolescence is simply a matter of developing active learning habits in your professional life. This leads us to Franklin's second managerial principle.

Franklin's Second Rule Of Management: All education is self-education.

Reading: Still The Key To Self-Education

As a business professor, I make it a point to read biographies of important people in business history in America and elsewhere. Many influential business managers are avid readers, a surprisingly common characteristic among such Digital Age luminaries as Ted Turner and Bill Gates. Even in our "paperless society," which boasts such varied educational media as video-based learning, experienced-based learning and Web-based learning, Gates still carves out two weeks every year for a private reading retreat in which he spends his days reading all the books he has set aside in the past year. In addition to this routine, Gates has acknowledged in interviews that he still tries to read books and magazines for an hour or so each day whenever possible.

Profiles of Genius by Gene Landrum features 13 business leaders who have made their mark since 1950 in America and abroad. Signs of self-education appear in almost all cases. Only six of the 13 finished college, and a number of the others never even finished high school. Yet it is not outrageous to label these individuals as geniuses. They learned a great deal about their world, but many did not rely on formal educational institutions for this knowledge. Rather, they developed lifelong habits of self-education, above all reading.

Benjamin Franklin Once Said ...

"Reading makes a full Man, Meditation a profound Man, discourse a clear Man."

OK, so I've said a great deal about the importance of reading. Yet Franklin suggests that reading is only one leg on the stool of self-education. The other two legs are meditation and discourse. These days, meditation is often associated with the Eastern concept of emptying your mind. But this is not the meditation that Franklin advocates. Rather than emptying our minds, Franklin challenges us to fill our minds through reading and then process what we have read. Yet this type of meditation is just as difficult as the concept of emptying the mind. It demands that we consider what we have read, put it in our own words, and possibly visit it again and again. I believe that Franklin wants us to view our minds as value-added information processors. Reading fills the mind, and meditation adds the value of personal perspective and experience. Meditation transforms information (a commodity) into knowledge (something personal and valuable).

Finally, Franklin challenges us to engage in discourse with other people about our newly discovered knowledge. This step is a safeguard against creating illusions by remaining in solitude. Through my own reading and meditation, I could mistakenly conclude that the key to business success is to always fly first class. If I share this idea in a social setting, the illusion is likely to be shattered. Further, if I share a quality piece of personal knowledge in a social setting, then I have the benefit of others' feedback that potentially adds even more value to my knowledge. Through proper social discourse, personal knowledge can be transformed into guiding wisdom.

Almost all 13 business leaders profiled by Landrum exhibited an intense love of reading and reliance on reading as a self-education tool. Tom Monaghan, founder of Domino's Pizza, was raised as an only child and spent a great deal of time reading at the library. The stories of P.T. Barnum, Abraham Lincoln and Frank Lloyd Wright were among his favorites, and he sought to imitate their rise from poor beginnings to prominence. Howard Head, who revolutionized skiing and tennis, counted reading Plato's dialogues and other philosophy writings among his favorite pastimes. William Lear, creator of the Lear jet, read an extraordinary number of books on electricity and technical innovations as a child. He also loved fiction populated by larger-than-life figures like Tom Swift and Horatio Alger's characters.

Akio Morita of Sony fame was also characterized as a serious reader of books on electronics and technology as a youth. His favorite? He states that *Popular Mechanics* changed his life. Arthur Jones, founder of the Nautilus Co., claimed to have read more by age 10 than most people read in a lifetime. Among his favorites were his father's medical library, Jonathan Swift, Edgar Allan Poe, Voltaire and Mark Twain. Finally, Ted Turner, father of modern cable television, started reading the Greek classics at an early age. His commitment to reading educated him about his heroes Alexander the Great, Attila the Hun and General George Patton.

Benjamin Franklin's success is attributed in part to his habit of reading, even though by today's standards, he may not have read many books. However, he began reading very early in his life, and his childhood home seemed to be an environment that encouraged reading and information gathering. Franklin's life suggests that how much you read may be less important than how rich the information is in what you read and how often you re-read it. Franklin returned again and again to the great books of his day and avoided the tabloids and tawdry ballads that were sold on the streets.

Learning From Board Games

In addition to reading, Franklin seemed to benefit a great deal from playing board games that encouraged the development of strategic thinking. In particular, late in his life he wrote a reflection, *The Morals*

Digging Your Own Well

Just because a book is old does not necessarily mean that its content is obsolete from a knowledge standpoint. All managers need a literary well that they can visit from time to time to find refreshment and inspiration. Franklin's personal library included not only current books on timely topics but also a great many classics. Among his favorites were Plutarch's Greek and Roman biographies and John Bunyan's *Pilgrim's Progress*, neither of which has anything to do with the direct management of a printing business. They can, however, provide a great deal of indirect managerial inspiration through their timeless examples of struggle and victory.

Burnout is a significant competitive threat in the current American economy that so highly rewards creativity and innovation. In such an environment, managers must take the lead in avoiding organizational burnout. One way is intentionally designing work to include the chance for refreshment and inspiration. The water cooler and coffee pot are staples of most office complexes, but refreshment goes well beyond biological thirst.

Constructing an elaborate office space decorated with expensive art and hiring string quartets to play background music would violate some fundamental Franklin management principles. Yet, managers can inexpensively allow employees to bring their own music into the workplace and decorate their workspaces with inspiring art. Going further, managers in urban communities can allow employees to take paid leave to visit a museum for an afternoon. In the same vein, it might be possible to allow "educational days" similar to "sick days" when employees specifically request time off for self-education. When employees take time off, encourage them to read great literature. What are you doing as a manager to dig a well for your thirsty employees?

of Chess, on the lessons he learned from playing chess. In that brief essay, Franklin describes life as a sort of chess game in which rational thinking and experience pay big dividends. He discussed three lessons that he learned from playing chess and applied them to daily life and business activity.

He called the first lesson *foresight*. That is, you are more likely to succeed in life and in business if you take time to consider both your own future activities as well as the future activities of your competitor. Even if your foresight is inaccurate, those who attempt it are more likely to survive and succeed than those who don't. A second lesson was that of *caution*. Both in chess and in life there are moves you make that you can't go back on. A little caution might save you from a lot of regret when choosing business partners, suppliers or workers. He called the final lesson *circumspection*. Circumspection simply means that you should consider the big picture before you make your move. Franklin suggests that it pays to look beyond your own narrow interests and consider other variables like your competitor's interests or how the legal environment might influence your activities.

Board games and competitive sports like tennis and auto racing have shaped the lives of businesspeople throughout American history. Many businessmen profiled by Gene Landrum described how competitive sports were central in shaping their views on business competition. Most people are familiar with Ted Turner's sailing exploits and his winning the America's Cup. Fewer people are familiar with how game-playing shaped the competitive thinking of the young Bill Gates. Biographers describe how the Gates family spent much of their leisure time playing competitive games and how Gates' grandmother made almost every activity a game when the family came over for a visit.

In my opinion, there's good news and bad news about competitive sports and games. The good news is they are a great self-education program for prospective businesspeople. Competitive games and sports can teach the benefits of foresight, caution and circumspection. Further, competition provides strong motivation for strengthening and sharpening our abilities. However, these same games can also foster some very dysfunctional thinking. The bad news is that too much competition can teach you that every encounter is a win-lose situation. Business is about mutually beneficial exchanges not one-sided victories, and the key is to keep your trading partners coming back to you. If they lose in every encounter with you, they are unlikely to return. I'll have more to say about that in Chapter 3.

A Club For Mutual Improvement

Another important self-education tactic used by Franklin was a circle of friends called the Junto (pronounced JUNE-tow). Franklin shares the story of the club's formation in his autobiography:

> "I should have mention'd before, that in the Autumn of the preceding Year I had form'd most of my ingenious Acquaintances into a Club for mutual Improvement, which we called the Junto. We met on Friday Evening. The Rules I drew up requir'd that every member in his Turn should produce one or more Queries on any Point of Morals, Politics or Natural Philosophy, to be discuss'd by the Company, and once in three Months produce & read an Essay of his own Writing on any Subject he pleased. Our Debates were to be under the Direction of a President, and to be conducted in the sincere Spirit of Inquiry after Truth, without Fondness for Dispute, or Desire of Victory; and to prevent Warmth all Expressions of Positiveness in Opinion or of direct Contradiction, were after some time made contraband & prohibited under small pecuniary Penalties."

A formal, structured gathering of like- and unlike-minded individuals can be one of the best self-education experiences you will ever have. Note that it's a *formal* and *structured* gathering. Franklin and his friends didn't just gather over coffee and doughnuts on Friday mornings and hope that something interesting would happen; such meetings tend to produce gossip more than useful information. Rather, like much of Franklin's life, he had a specific plan for the self-education activity known as the Junto. Let's take a closer look at the elements that intentionally contributed to the educational success of the Junto.

● **Designated meeting time:** Franklin and his friends cleared their calendars each Friday evening for the meeting of the Junto. The group showed a remarkable amount of longevity and met continually from its inception in the fall of 1727 until 1757—30 years! I've been part of a number of small groups that began with noble aspirations and fizzled out after less than a year of meetings. It's a testament to Franklin's commitment to self-education that the Junto lasted as long as it did.

● **Careful selection of a limited membership:** The Junto was a secret and exclusive club. Exclusive is a not a popular word in today's world of inclusiveness. Yet, the Junto was formed to provide a forum for poor, young, enterprising businessmen who were excluded from the more established and expensive merchants' club. The size of the Junto was limited to 12 members and remained so for three decades despite the temptation to increase the group as its influence grew. The group was composed entirely of young, male tradesmen, but the members exhibited a remarkable diversity in their interests: four printers, a surveyor, a copier of deeds and poetry lover, a mathematician, a shoemaker, a mechanic, a clerk, an Oxford scholar, and a wealthy landowner. The diversity of intellectual talents contributed to the educational impact the meetings had on Franklin.

- **Clear purpose and structure for meetings:** The Junto met for one main purpose: the mutual improvement of the members. Aside from the questions addressed in "Fuel For The Junto's Engine" on page 25, the members of the Junto were expected to take turns preparing essays on points of morals, politics, philosophy and subjects of their own interest. The essay was read aloud in the meeting, and a debate ensued that was presided over by an appointed president.

- **Opportunity to express opinions:** The Junto existed to provide its members a place to air their opinions and get feedback on them. The rules of conversation clearly stated that each member in his turn was responsible for developing a position paper prior to coming to the meeting. (A position paper is simply an essay promoting or opposing an issue in politics, philosophy or other field.) At the meeting, the essays would be shared, and the other members of the Junto would critique the opinion without trying to start a dispute. Further, extreme statements of agreement or disagreement were banned and fined. The result was a place where friends could gather and sharpen their views on important matters in a nonthreatening and highly educational environment.

- **Clear rules and penalties:** Ever the person to believe in the power of incentives, Franklin was also wise enough to outline a few rules and penalties to govern the behavior of members. As a general rule, conversation in the Junto was to be undertaken with a ". . . sincere spirit of inquiry after truth." Although the autobiography never gives a definitive account of the other rules governing the Junto, it appears that penalties existed for tardiness, absenteeism, being too contradictory, being too agreeable and being unprepared. Not surprisingly, all penalties were monetary fines.

Fuel For The Junto's Engine

1 n addition to the formal structure governing the Junto that's discussed here, Franklin and his friends had a list of questions that governed the conversation at each meeting of the Junto. Below, I've modified a number of Franklin's original list of questions to fit a modern context. If you continue your education using the methods established by Franklin, you might consider asking some or all of these questions at your meetings:

- Have you recently read anything or seen any programming that you found remarkable or suitable to be communicated to this group?

- Have you recently heard of any failed businesses, and what were the causes?

- Have you recently encountered any successful businesses, and why do you think they are succeeding?

- Have you recently experienced any problems in your business and, if so, how did you solve them?

- Have you noticed any inadequacy or limitation in existing laws, or have you heard of a beneficial legislative bill that might need to be supported?

- Do you know any new business owners whom we should help and encourage?

- Have you lately heard any member of our group's reputation attacked?

- Are you struggling with any decisions in which you think the advice of the group might be of service?

The Modern-Day Junto

The general principles governing Franklin's Junto can easily be applied to the modern business context. Just because something involves a group doesn't mean that it's not self-education. The key to self-education is personal initiative rather than doing everything (as my

3-year-old son would say) "all by myself." Franklin believed that if you learned only from yourself, you had a fool for a teacher. He believed that a good social network was essential to self-education. This is equally true for our modern business context. All managers need friends and colleagues with whom they can exchange ideas, test new concepts, and challenge and improve their own knowledge base. The odds of being a self-educator go up when you have some form of social accountability.

Here are a few suggestions for making this work in the modern business context. Start with a group of fellow managers or business owners. Even if all of you have the same job, strive for a diversity of backgrounds within the group to stimulate conversation. Next, set a designated meeting time and try to avoid meeting over lunch. Although dining provides a wonderful social atmosphere, it most likely will detract from self-education.

Once you have the membership selected and the time established, draw up a set of guidelines to structure the conversation. By definition, the Junto will meet for mutual self-improvement. However, the topics and structure of the conversation are up to the participants. You may want to talk over recent trends affecting your industry. Maybe the conversation will revolve around editorials in popular business magazines, and you might start writing your own editorials. Maybe you'll convene to talk about a literary classic like *Moby Dick* or *Atlas Shrugged*. Whatever you do, it is important to establish a ritual and a structure that can be followed each week to keep the group on task and moving forward together. If nothing else, just fall back on the structure outlined above that Franklin and his friends used.

A word of caution should accompany an educational plan like this. Adam Smith warned in *The Wealth of Nations* that businesspeople rarely gather together under one roof without the talk turning toward price fixing and collusion against the public good. As a result, a cloud of suspicion will always hang over any meeting involving businesspeople from different companies. Before his retirement, my father was one of the most conscientious businessmen I've known. Yet, he and some other businessmen in town attracted the attention of the state attorney general because they met every so often for coffee at a local cafe. They went to the same church and also talked about church business over coffee. The attorney general thought otherwise and demanded that they stop meeting.

Given such long-standing suspicions about business, it's probably advisable to avoid meeting too regularly with individuals from competing firms. Should you expand your group membership beyond your own firm, the best defense is to choose a diverse group from unrelated businesses and keep informal records of all meetings. Following Franklin's example, keep the conversation structured and focused on mutual self-improvement rather than collusive self-enrichment.

Good Sense Is Better Than Good Sound

Being a celebrity has its drawbacks. In July 1993, the town of Ismay, Montana, changed its name to Joe, Montana, to honor the well-known quarterback Joe Montana, who had then just signed to play for the Kansas City Chiefs. As a result of the publicity, civic leaders admitted to netting nearly $70,000 during the next seven months to fund the local volunteer fire department. Things were no different two centuries ago. In fact, there are more towns in America named Franklin than any other name.

In 1778, the town of Exeter, Massachusetts, was incorporated after splitting off from its neighbor, Wrentham. Exeter promptly changed its name to Franklin, but not without an ulterior motive. The farmers of rural Exeter conducted all civic, government, social, cultural and religious activities in the local church. The church, however, had no bell with which to summon the townspeople for meetings or to sound a warning for fire or attack.

With high hopes, the town leaders changed the name of the town and wrote to Benjamin Franklin informing him of this great honor. They also humbly requested him to donate a bell to hang in the local church. Much to their surprise, Franklin was not so inclined. Instead of a bell, Franklin sent the farmers a crate of books and suggested they start a library. His reason was that "sense" was always preferable to "sound." The farmers took his suggestion for the library, and the books Franklin donated are still on public display in the Franklin Public Library.

The Self-Educating Company

Every business must do two basic things to ensure survival. First, all workers in a business must act in a coordinated fashion. That is, everybody must move in the same general direction for a business to compete effectively. Second, businesses must adapt to changing environments to survive, and adaptation comes only through the actions of people. These may be relatively obvious maxims, but the failure to implement them has brought down many a business. I'm not just playing word games with the well-known buzzword "the learning organization." Rather, I'm convinced that learning is really more a matter of self-educating individuals than self-educating institutions. The idea of "the learning organization" is that it's more a matter of reinventing the structure and culture of the company than looking for solutions at the level of the individual employee. This chapter has plenty of examples of self-educating individuals. I want to close with two examples from companies that have done a great deal to promote self-education.

First, let's see how self-education can coordinate the activities of a company and get workers moving in the same general direction. The CEO of People Express Airlines, Don Burr, wanted to create an organizational culture in which workers could easily understand and communicate to others. Simply put, he wanted to create the self-educating business. To do so, he threw out the rule books and boiled down company policy to six basic precepts:

1. Service, commitment to the growth and development of our people

2. To be the best provider of air transportation

3. To provide the highest quality of leadership

4. To serve as a role model for others

5. Simplicity

6. Maximization of profits

Burr then incorporated these six guiding precepts into a one-page document called "Leadership is Everything." Anybody wanting to make a culturally correct decision at People Express had only to recall these six guidelines and the information on the single-page policy manual—a very simple thing to do—and then apply them to the situation at hand. Burr's genius in this undertaking was not to avoid rules altogether but to create a system of broad, easy-to-remember guidelines that every employee could recall and pass on to others. Planning for every contingency is not the most effective way to develop company policy. Complexity can paralyze where simplicity can set employees free—and Burr's greatest achievement as a manager was giving his workers a great deal of freedom.

Whereas the key to coordination might be focusing all workers on making culturally correct decisions, the key to adaptation is most

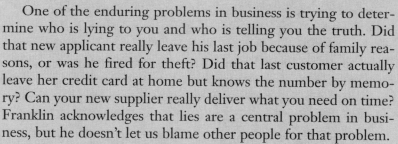

Benjamin Franklin Once Said ...

"Who has deceiv'd thee so oft as thyself?"

One of the enduring problems in business is trying to determine who is lying to you and who is telling you the truth. Did that new applicant really leave his last job because of family reasons, or was he fired for theft? Did that last customer actually leave her credit card at home but knows the number by memory? Can your new supplier really deliver what you need on time? Franklin acknowledges that lies are a central problem in business, but he doesn't let us blame other people for that problem.

Franklin suggests that we should look to ourselves first to shatter the illusions that plague us in the marketplace. One of the fastest ways to shatter illusions is to share your thoughts with friends in an environment dedicated to mutual self-improvement. When the Junto met, all members were challenged to put their opinions to the test of rational discourse. I'd gamble to say that the members of the Junto left with fewer illusions and fewer prejudices. Our illusions and prejudices cannot stand the scrutiny of social interaction.

Another way we deceive ourselves is through our own desperation. We tend to believe in anything when our backs are against the wall. Franklin's commitment to creating abundant business environments helped keep illusion in check. When you have options and your own set of priorities, you're less likely to fall for the lies that some will try to sell you.

likely maximizing operational information. A great example of an organization that learns as it goes is the Granite Rock Company of Watsonville, California. A fairly mundane business by Digital Age standards, the company produces and sells crushed rock, concrete and asphalt and has a paving operation. However, it's a model of responsiveness for many more technologically sophisticated firms.

The management at Granite Rock is committed to providing workers with what they call a flood of information from customers, the competitive environment, and the firm's own operations. The basic assumption is that workers with good information will make good survival choices. Granite Rock has also created a company with a bias for action. Information empowers activity, so Granite Rock grouped workers in highly visible problem-solving teams in which workers hold one another accountable for taking action on information to solve pressing competitive problems. The only rule: Follow the solution wherever it may lead. This guideline allows for maximum adaptation and doesn't make problem-solving employees a slave to static strategic plans. Finally, Granite Rock provides a great deal more training per employee than the standard mining company and allows for nontraditional career movement. It's not uncommon for people in finance and accounting to have gotten their start with the company by working in the quarries.

It's my hope that the examples in these two companies and the example of Franklin's Junto prompt you to think seriously about self-education. As the rate of change in society continues to advance and information technology continues to improve, knowledge and skills will be obsolete more and more quickly. Without a plan for self-education, you'll be forced to rely on the generosity of others to help you keep up. Franklin knew that this was folly. As a result, he left a useful self-education example that all can imitate.

What Good Shall I Do This Day?

❑ Admit that your skills and knowledge are becoming obsolete.

❑ Develop a daily habit of reading. Start with something in which you are most interested, but try to move beyond news magazines and sports pages and into richer sources.

❑ Instead of spending the evening watching television alone, consider playing games with your children or friends. Try to choose games where success depends upon strategic thinking rather than luck.

❑ Develop your own Junto at work. For members, choose people within your own business.

❑ Structure these meetings so they work for a purpose. Otherwise, they are likely to devolve into gossip sessions.

❑ Begin the habit of developing and stating your views in the Junto. Allow your friends there to critique your views, and use their feedback to sharpen your ideas and eliminate your illusions.

❑ Remove information barriers in your firm, and start a flood of information aimed toward your workers. Closed-book management is less and less competitive.

❑ Increase your training budgets and require all workers to seek 40 hours of training per year. Let them choose their own program of education. Don't turn down any reasonable request.

❑ If something is particularly important at your firm, make the message so simple that it can quickly and easily be taught to all newcomers.

At New York I found my Friend Collins, who had arriv'd there some Time before me. We had been intimate from Children, and had read the same Books together. But he had the Advantage of more time for reading, & Studying and a wonderful Genius for Mathematical Learning in which he far outstripped me. While I liv'd in Boston most of my Hours of Leisure for Conversation were spent with him, & he continu'd a sober as well as industrious Lad; was much respected for his Learning by several of the Clergy & other Gentlemen, & seemed to promise making a good Figure in Life: but during my Absence he had acquir'd a Habit of Sotting with Brandy; and I found by his own Account & what I heard from others, that he had been drunk every day since his Arrival at new York, & behaved very oddly. He had gam'd too and lost his Money, so that I was oblig'd to discharge his Lodgings, & defray his Expenses to and at Philadelphia: Which prov'd extremely inconvenient to me.

—Benjamin Franklin
discussing the downward spiral
of a childhood friend

Chapter 3

How To Manage Others Effectively

ore and more people are arriving late to work, and it's starting to become a problem. When you took the job as manager at the insurance claims processing center a year ago,
you had been handed a department that ran perfectly. The employees
knew their jobs, everybody was comfortable with the work and vacation schedules, and you were excited about your first job as a manager.

Things kept running well for a while, but then you started to notice some slippage. Every now and then an employee or two would arrive a little later than normal, but they always seemed to have a ready
excuse for why they were late. "My daughter was sick today, and I had
to arrange for some care before I left home." You couldn't argue with
that one. As a single mother, you know the burdens of parenting and
earning a living at the same time. In fact, your own children had de-

layed your arrival to work on a number of occasions since you took this job. "I had to finish a couple of cigarettes before I came in" was starting to become another popular excuse. It's the one you heard this morning that made you stop in your tracks: "Well, you're late to work almost as much as anybody else here."

That was the kind of comment that made you want to strike back and strike back hard with your managerial authority. What right did that staff member have to question you? You could fire the whole lot of them if you saw fit. Well, not all of them, but you have some pretty good dirt on a few of them. You go out to lunch alone today and take a mental inventory of the past year. You're late to work because of some child-related problem about once a month. Also, a car wreck or unexpected road construction probably delays your arrival about once a month, too. Then there are the 7 a.m. staff meetings every Monday with your boss and peers at the office across town. They're usually finished by the 8 a.m. starting time for your department. Anyway, it's completely excusable to arrive late when you're coming from another company-related event. Or is it? Altogether, you've probably arrived late to work five or six times per month. Let's see, there are about 22 working days in a month, and you're late, say, 25 percent of the time. That's about what your workers are averaging. Maybe the best way to fix this is to crack down on it immediately.

Managing In The Fishbowl

Many managers underestimate the power and influence of their social example both on their peers and the workers they supervise. Like it or not, all managers ultimately manage "from the fishbowl," meaning that their actions and reactions are closely watched by everybody who reports to them. When everybody looks to you as the most powerful social example in the office, you're in need of Franklin's next management principle.

Franklin's Third Rule Of Management:
Seek first to manage yourself, then to manage others.

Benjamin Franklin Once Said ...

"Well done is better than well said."

"A good Example is the best sermon."

For almost 2,000 years, sermons have been central to communicating moral instruction in hopes of improving behavior. Franklin was a leading advocate of people changing their behavior for the better. However, he believed that setting a good example was better moral instruction than preaching sermons.

Franklin well understood the concept of managing from the fishbowl. The cubicles of today's offices would seem private by comparison with the printing houses in which he worked. Every movement and every activity could be watched and judged by others working in the shop. In this environment, Franklin took great care to set a positive and powerful social example for his fellow workers. Franklin enjoyed a great deal of influence among his fellow workers and fellow citizens as a result of his commitment to self-management.

In the example above, the manager struggling to get late-arriving employees under control would most likely find that a crackdown on them would create a nasty backlash. She must first seek to get her own pattern of arriving late under control before she will have any credibility among the workers and any success in correcting their behavior. Franklin would have suggested that a manager who sets a powerfully good social example can solve most workplace problems before they appear. Then, when a problem arises, the manager has her own good example to point to when employees suggest that she is asking them to do the impossible.

A Little Bit Of Word Play

The importance of self-management is not a clear and present theme in Franklin's autobiography. In fact, he never even uses the term to describe his own behavior. However, Franklin's ability to manage himself was foundational to almost everything he accomplished. The closest Franklin ever came to referring to self-management was in some of the sayings found in *Poor Richard's Almanac*. In 1734, Franklin professed through *Poor Richard*, "If you be revenged of your enemy, govern your self," and in 1750 he said, "He is a Governor that governs his passions and he is a servant that serves them."

In the opening quotation for this chapter, Franklin details the downward spiral of an otherwise talented friend who failed completely in the area of self-management. His friend Collins seemed to have many advantages over Franklin in intelligence and study. Yet Collins lost all those advantages when he gambled and drank heavily. There's no doubt in my mind that Franklin learned from such negative examples.

The principles of this chapter—self-management—and the previous chapter—self-education—have masqueraded under the labels "self-help" and "self-improvement" for most of the 20th century. These phrases are modern manifestations of the more powerful underlying principles of self-education and self-management that Franklin demonstrates again and again in his autobiography. Self-education is a more powerful idea than self-improvement because self-improvement offers only a "quick fix." Self-education focuses more on developing a lifelong learning habit to help you continually adapt to changing environments. Whereas self-help suggests an individual focus, self-management points to more foundational social and organizational effects of personal excellence on the part of managers. The drinking and gambling problems experienced by Franklin's friend Collins need more than a "quick fix." Collins needs self-management, not just some superficial self-improvement.

Swimming Lessons (Or Is That Lessons From Swimming?)

One thing to constantly keep in mind about Franklin is that he excelled in a wide variety of endeavors—politician, scientist, inventor and even athlete—and he benefited greatly from them all. Franklin is not remembered as an athlete, but swimming was apparently a favorite sport. He learned to swim early in life because his family lived near water. Later, when he moved to London to work in the printing industry, he continued swimming and refined this leisure-time activity.

Franklin writes about a trip on a river in England with some companions. One of them was familiar with Franklin's swimming abilities and convinced him to jump into the river to demonstrate these skills. Franklin swam in the river for nearly three and a half miles,

> ". . . performing on the Way many Feats of Activity both upon & under the Water, that surpris'd & pleas'd those to whom they were Novelties. I had from a Child been ever delighted with this Exercise, had studied & practis'd all Thevenot's Motions & Positions, added some of my own, aiming at the graceful & easy, as well as the Useful. All these I took this Occasion of exhibiting to the Company, & was much flatter'd by their Admiration."

Wait a minute: Who is this Thevenot fellow, and what are his "Motions & Positions"? Thevenot wrote *The Art of Swimming: Illustrated by Proper Figures*, a book that Franklin apparently studied intently as a youth. The sport of swimming in those days consisted not only of learning not to sink but also of a variety of aesthetically pleasing positions to demonstrate for spectators—something like solo synchronized swimming. As unlikely as it seems, there's a good chance Franklin learned some of his most important management lessons from swimming.

As mentioned in Chapter 2, people learn important lessons from participating in sports. Isn't that how we justify most of the athletic programs in American public education? We say something like, "Oh, think of the lessons the children will learn in teamwork and how to lose gracefully." Franklin's athletic endeavors were fundamentally different from our current thinking in many important ways. First, our current sports are team-based. Second, and more important, they are competitive—an individual or team faces an opponent—and there is a winner and a loser in the end.

Franklin's sport of choice differed from much of our current athletic activity in three key ways. First, swimming was not a team-based sport. Rather, you only had to master yourself to be a swimmer. Second, individuals did not compete directly with one another. Thus, there were no winners or losers. Finally, personal acclaim was possible and could be achieved by being more and more creative in the positions and moves exhibited while swimming before an audience.

The best modern-day analogy for Franklin's swimming activity is the group of sports collectively known as the X Games. The X Games are extreme sports, and they include skateboarding, snowboarding, rock climbing, in-line skating and stunt biking. Give me a chance to explain why I would compare a group of young, risk-taking, body-pierced extremists with Benjamin Franklin.

Most of our current team-based sports ultimately teach two key lessons. First, the goals of the team come before personal goals. Second, victory is achieved by either power or deception. Victory by power is having more talent than your competitors and literally running over them on the way to the goal line. Victory by deception occurs when you make your opponent think you're doing one thing while you're really doing another—faking a run and throwing a pass, faking a bunt and hitting a single, or faking a pump then shooting a basket.

A Means To An End

Franklin's willingness to manage himself first was perhaps rooted in his love of liberty and independence. In the end, the government exists primarily to protect us from the damage other people can do to our lives. A government is most necessary when people are extremely dishonest. For example, the more thieves and con artists in a population, the more the government is justified in growing larger to keep such negative forces in the population from exploiting good citizens.

Franklin did not like centralized power, and he especially kept a close watch on governments. It's reasonable to assume that Franklin may have promoted his ideas of self-management to the general population to help keep the growth of government in check. The more willing the people are to manage their own behavior, the less they need the federal government to manage their affairs for them. For example, businesspeople in a monopoly should not charge all the market can bear because it creates an invitation for government to intervene and regulate. Are you tired of big government? Try managing yourself and teaching others to manage themselves to promote liberty and independence the Franklin way.

Extreme sports teach two entirely different lessons. The first is that victory is achieved through individual excellence. You submit to no one, and there's no team goal. Thus, these sports are heavy on individual responsibility and effort. A second lesson in extreme sports is that creativity, rather than deception, leads to victory. You differentiate yourself from the competition by being more creative in a tournament or ranking. It's not a traditional win or loss.

Consider these two lessons from the entrepreneurial business training point of view. Would you rather have employees socialized to power, deception and taking orders, or skilled in individual responsibility and creativity? The future entrepreneurs of this nation are more likely to emerge from extreme sports than from traditional sports.

Everyone Is A Manager

The world needs managers. Isn't that good news for management fans? The world needs individuals in organizations who set goals, monitor results and determine priorities. Now for the interesting twist: Anybody can do this. Everybody can ultimately *become* the manager of his or her own work and life. If you never learn to manage yourself, somebody else will always be managing you—a parent, the government or a workplace manager.

Self-managing employees are the key to a flat organization. People Express Airlines used self-management as part of determining who would be asked to work for the company. People Express CEO Don Burr expressed it best by saying, "Everyone is a manager at People Express." That airline didn't have the resources or the time to build a traditional hierarchy in which one set of workers watches over another set of workers and so on. Rather, they just found as many self-managing people as they could and hired them. They ended up with about one hire for every 100 applicants. Genuinely self-managing workers are few and far between—but they are out there!

Self-Management At Nucor Steel

Nucor Steel is one of the great American business success stories of the late 20th century. Nucor produces steel in technologically sophisticated mini-mills that can be capitalized for 10 percent to 15 percent of what integrated steel firms like USX or Bethlehem Steel would spend building a plant. Nucor is one of the few firms that ate their competitors. Nucor's mini-mills make steel from scrap metal. During Big Steel's decline in the late 1980s and early 1990s, Nucor bought scrap metal, including pieces of old buildings and machinery, from larger, integrated competitors, melted it in their mini-mills, and sold it for money.

Central to Nucor's success is its commitment to a self-managing organization, beginning with the staffing and selection process. Plant managers administer a psychological test to prospective employees that aims to identify self-reliant, goal-oriented people. Self-management traits take precedence over other factors such as previous steel-making experience. Self-starting employees are then placed in an operational environment in which productivity is handsomely rewarded with money.

This self-managing foundation allowed Nucor to operate with only five layers of management between the mill worker and the CEO of the company (mill worker-foreman-department head-plant manager-COO-CEO). Furthermore, the majority of the management is at the plant level. In contrast to the dozen or so layers of management at Nucor's integrated competitors, a flatter organiza-

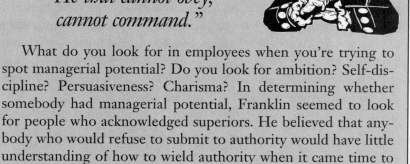

Benjamin Franklin Once Said . . .

"He that cannot obey, cannot command."

What do you look for in employees when you're trying to spot managerial potential? Do you look for ambition? Self-discipline? Persuasiveness? Charisma? In determining whether somebody had managerial potential, Franklin seemed to look for people who acknowledged superiors. He believed that anybody who would refuse to submit to authority would have little understanding of how to wield authority when it came time to do so. Authority structures are a fact of life. Franklin reminds us that there will always be somebody to whom you must answer.

tion presents quite a cost saving and allows for rapid response to emergent opportunities.

It almost seems that Nucor is attempting to build an organization that doesn't need any management at all. That is most likely impossible, but Nucor's initial assumptions about the value of self-managing operations have given them a remarkable competitive advantage. Management is necessary in any organization to set direction and to maintain momentum. However, the more employees who can do this for themselves, the fewer managers you will need.

How Do You Spot A Self-Manager?

So, how exactly do you go about hiring self-managing employees? As mentioned above, Nucor Steel uses a psychological test, but since the test isn't available for public purchase, you will have to find another way. If you're interested in using paper-and-pencil psychological tests, you might want to use the *Self Reliance Inventory*, a test which attempts to measure people who are comfortable and capable of working alone but are able to depend on others when appropriate. (For purchase information, contact Janice Joplin at Southern Illinois University, 618-453-3328). The *Self Management Assessment Questionnaire* might be useful as well; it was designed to evaluate people on 10 dimensions that characterize excellent self-managers. These dimensions include management of time and resources, looking to the future, and setting high goals. (For purchase information, contact Marshall Sashkin at Ducochon Press, P.O. Box 620, Seabrook, MD 20706-0620, 301-552-9523.)

As a former recruiter, one of my favorite techniques is behavior-based interviewing. The basic idea underlying this technique is that past performance is the best predictor of future performance. In behavior-based interviewing, job applicants are asked What have you done? rather than Who are you? As such, a good behavior-based interview should probe an applicant's past successes and work habits. To give you some idea of how this works, here are some questions that explore past habits and behavior patterns:

● What habits have you developed during your professional life to manage your time and resources?

● Tell me about your personal goal-setting process.

Are You A Self-Manager?

Are you wondering if you're a self-manager? You may already know the answer, but if you don't, here's a list of questions adapted from the *Self Management Assessment Questionnaire*. If you answer "Yes" to most of them, then you're well on your way to becoming a self-manager.

- During the day, do I often think of what it will be like when I achieve my goals?
- When I decide to take a risk with another person, am I absolutely committed to follow through?
- Do I try to learn new things and meet new people outside work?
- Do I allocate specific time and resources for each of my work projects?
- Do my goals include people close to me?
- Do I feel fortunate to be living at this time in history?
- Do I try to plan for the effects of long-range trends?
- Do I rehearse in my mind the exact details of my anticipated achievements at work?

- Think of a time when you had to make a decision without all the relevant information or input from your superiors. How did you go about making that decision?
- Let's assume that someone accuses you of being lazy and undirected. What evidence would you offer to counter such an accusation?

The Danger Of Being An Effective Self-Manager

Being a self-managing individual is not without its drawbacks. In fact, an incident from Franklin's life well illustrates the political problems that can arise when you promote self-management throughout a company. Franklin was such a capable manager that his employer at one time, Samuel Keimer, concluded that the printing house could run just fine without Franklin's presence, which was a great compliment to Franklin but a great mistake on Keimer's part. Keimer ended up killing the goose that laid the golden egg. Franklin notes the incident in his autobiography:

> "With the rest [of the workers] I began to live agreeably; for they all respected me, the more as they found Keimer incapable of instructing them, and that from me they learned something daily. But however serviceable I might be, I found that my Services became every Day of less importance, as the other Hands improv'd in the Business. And when Keimer paid my second Quarter's Wages, he let me know that he felt them too heavy, and thought I should make an Abatement. He grew by degrees less civil, put on more of the Master, frequently found Fault, was captious and seem'd ready for an Out-breaking."

The root of the problem was Keimer's own insecurity, evidenced by a great deal of envy toward Franklin. Franklin's success in managing himself and genuinely empowering the other workers posed a threat to Keimer as master of the print shop. As a result, he hinted to Franklin that his job might not be too secure in the future. Keimer began looking for reasons to get rid of Franklin at this point, and a petty incident ended their relationship. Read on as Franklin recounts the story:

> "At length a Trifle snapped our Connection. For a great Noise happening near the Courthouse, I put my Head out of the Window to see what was the Matter. Keimer being in the Street look'd up & saw me, call'd out to me in a loud voice and angry Tone to mind my Business, adding some reproachful Words that nettled me the more for their Publicity, all the Neighbors who were looking out on the same Occasion being Witnesses to how I was treated. He came up immediately into the Printing-house, continu'd the Quarrel, high Words pass'd on both Sides, he gave me the Quarter's Warning we had stipulated, expressing a Wish that he had not been oblig'd to so long a Warning. I told him his wish was unnecessary for I would leave him that Instant; and so taking my Hat walk'd out of Doors . . ."

How would you like to be known in history as the manager who fired Benjamin Franklin? The lessons from this incident cut two ways.

First, everyone who aspires to becoming a self-manager needs to be aware that envy is alive and well in the workplace. As you succeed and as others succeed because you have empowered them, some of your peers may strike back if they feel that your success makes them look bad.

Second, managers need to learn from Keimer's bad example. A manager should not feel threatened when workers start managing themselves. Rather than eliminating the need for managers, self-managing workers actually change the nature of the manager's job. Managers are liberated from the role of motivator and scorekeeper and can concentrate more on such activities as growing the business and building up external contacts.

What Good Shall I Do This Day?

❏ Resolve today to become a powerful social example for others to follow. A good example is still the best sermon.

❏ Learn additional self-management skills in the school of non-competitive sports. Try to take up swimming, rock-climbing or even yoga.

❏ Help other people learn how to become self-managers. This will give you and others greater freedom.

❏ Start identifying self-managers as part of your recruiting process.

❏ Don't be surprised if creating self-managers results in a backlash. Defend yourself by pointing to the positive results.

And as the chief Ends of Conversation are to inform, or to be informed, to please or to persuade, *I wish well-meaning sensible Men would not lessen their Power of doing Good by a Positive assuming Manner that seldom fails to disgust, tends to create Opposition, and to defeat every one of those Purposes for which Speech was given us, to wit, giving or receiving Information, or Pleasure: For if you would inform, a positive dogmatical Manner of advancing your Sentiments, may provoke Contradiction & prevent a candid Attention. If you wish Information & Improvement from the Knowledge of others and yet at the same time express yourself as firmly fix'd in your present Opinions, modest sensible Men, who do not love Disputation, will probably leave you undisturb'd in the Possession of your Error; and by such a Manner you can seldom hope to recommend yourself in pleasing your Hearers, or to persuade those whose Concurrence you desire.*

—Benjamin Franklin
describing why rigid opinions
ultimately fail to persuade

Chapter 4

Winning
In The End

ou're driving home from work late one Thursday afternoon when—*bam!*—lightning strikes! You've just had a burst of inspiration . . . a brainstorm. Things are going well at work, but you're constantly looking for ways to put your work team over the top. Now, you think you have just the thing: competitive team sports. You loved competing in team sports in high school, and you've heard a number of your co-workers talk about their glory days in high school and even college-level athletics.

As you drive, your mind wanders to your fondest sports memories. You remember the time you did the perfect fake and left the defender standing there while you scored. You've been faking them all out ever since, you think to yourself. And those great sports rivalries! You lived every year for the big game against the high school across town. To this day, you hate their colors. You glance at the speedometer and realize that you've been speeding down the freeway, just thinking about competition. You start weaving in and out of the cars around you. A few of them honk at you, and you laugh with enjoyment. "Yes sir," you think to yourself, "I learned some great lessons from sports, and it's time we started doing the same at work!"

America is a nation of competitors, and one of the great myths of any competitive society is that to win overall, you have to win every interaction along the way. Isn't America the nation that coined the phrase, Winning isn't everything; it's the only thing? In Franklin's view, winning was extremely important, but he defined winning a little differently. For Franklin, winning consisted of more than coming out on top in some battle of wills or words. Rather, winning demanded sowing the seeds of influence and goodwill that could be reaped at some future point.

Franklin's Fourth Rule Of Management:
Influence is more important than victory.

Rule #1: Be Nice

In 1984, Robert Axelrod, a political scientist at the University of Michigan, published a controversial little book called *The Evolution of Cooperation*. It was basically a research monologue describing a computer-based tournament that Axelrod conducted among a group of social scientists. Axelrod challenged the best minds in the nation to come up with a solution for a difficult social situation in which you could be taken advantage of if you were too trustworthy. The game was easily scored, and Axelrod requested that all contestants write their solutions as computer programs to be played against each another in a round-robin tournament.

The entries were widely varied. Some complex programs sought to predict all an opponent's possible moves and choose a response to maximize the end score. Some rather devious programs were designed to take advantage of trusting opponents. Random programs were designed to confuse players into making rational responses to irrational activities. And one program, the shortest entry, was only four lines long. It was called Tit-for-Tat, and it won the tournament.

Tit-for-Tat's strategy for navigating this treacherous social situation boiled down to four suggestions. First, be nice. In other words, never be the first to pick a fight in any situation. Niceness prevents you from getting into unnecessary trouble. Second, be retaliatory

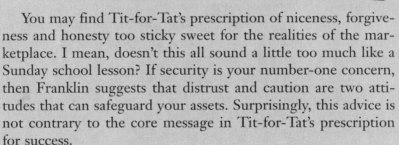

Benjamin Franklin Once Said ...

"Distrust & caution are the
parents of security."

You may find Tit-for-Tat's prescription of niceness, forgiveness and honesty too sticky sweet for the realities of the marketplace. I mean, doesn't this all sound a little too much like a Sunday school lesson? If security is your number-one concern, then Franklin suggests that distrust and caution are two attitudes that can safeguard your assets. Surprisingly, this advice is not contrary to the core message in Tit-for-Tat's prescription for success.

First, Tit-for-Tat uses a fundamentally pessimistic strategy. It assumes that somebody somewhere will try to take the money and run. Therefore, it's ready to retaliate when necessary. We've learned that strategies that are eager to cooperate but unwilling to retaliate fall prey to crafty exploiters.

Another key to Tit-for-Tat's long-term effectiveness is its cautiousness. By cooperating on the first move, it gave everybody it met the chance to be good. If the other party did not cooperate, then Tit-for-Tat began to retaliate until the other party signaled a willingness to cooperate once again. Being cautious is not about avoiding risk but taking reasonable risks. Putting all your assets on the table is pretty dumb. However, putting a little on the table to see if the other party shakes your hand or slaps it is a prudent, cautious move.

when necessary. A willingness to punish players who try to take advantage of you quickly discourages others from doing the same. Third, be forgiving when asked. A willingness to forgive a breach of trust by another player seemed to be the quickest route to restoring a mutually beneficial relationship. Finally, be totally clear about your intentions. Clarity makes you intelligible to the other players and builds trust quicker than more deceptive strategies.

Benjamin Franklin Once Said ...

"Those that have much Business must have much Pardon."

Franklin was a strong advocate for a world of justice where everybody got what they earned—good or bad. He was also an advocate of pardon, or letting people off the hook when they deserved to be punished. In fact, he suggests that pardon may be one of your best business policies.

Franklin lived and worked in an environment heavily influenced by Puritan culture. He most likely dealt with many people who believed that they were "sinners in the hands of an angry God" and, therefore, in desperate need of pardon to feel good about themselves. As a businessman, Franklin may have capitalized on this need for mercy by creating a business environment that gave people second and third chances. Franklin also knew that people often fail to repay debts, keep promises and meet deadlines. Rather than writing them off at the time of the first offense, he suggested pardoning them. The likely result was increased loyalty and repeat business.

Like Franklin, Tit-for-Tat also suggests that forgiveness pays excellent dividends. Those strategies that forgave prior offenses and gave people the opportunity to continue trading profited handsomely in the long run. Pardon may just be one of the best managerial policies you can have. It can very well motivate people toward taking more risks. But don't throw justice out the window. Pardon is meaningless and powerless in a world without justice.

Some counterintuitive results for managers fell out of Axelrod's tournament. First, the key to success in competitive environments is the ability to elicit cooperation. Many players approached the tournament with the attitude that strategies which more effectively exploit opponents' weaknesses would win. Such strategies not only failed to win, but they were ineffective in the long run because they depended on gullible prey willing to put up with exploitation.

A second counterintuitive result from the tournament was that clarity, rather than deception, pays big dividends. Tit-for-Tat was very clear in its message of rewarding cooperation, and players looking for cooperative partners could test its promises in just a few moves. Finally, the last bit of good news from Axelrod's tournament is that the least complex strategy won. The key to success is *not* in exceedingly complex strategies that take every contingency into account.

Franklin's life suggests two key influences that helped shape his attitudes about competition and victory. First, he was exposed to the Socratic method early in life. Second, he tried to love his enemies rather than destroy them. Let's take a closer look at both of these concepts.

Resolving Conflicts The Really Old-Fashioned Way

Franklin was exposed to the Greek philosophers and historians. Among his favorite reading was anything demonstrating the Socratic method. He writes,

> "While I was intent on improving my Language, I met with an English Grammar (I think it was Greenwood's) at the End of which there were two little Sketches of the Arts of Rhetoric and Logic, the latter finishing with a Specimen of a Dispute in the Socratic Method. And soon after I procur'd Xenophon's *Memorable Things of Socrates*, wherein there are many Instances of the same Method. I was charm'd with it, adopted it, dropped my abrupt Contradiction, and positive Argumentation, and put on the humble Inquirer & Doubter."

What exactly is the Socratic method? Most people believe that a Socratic dialogue is when a professor asks questions to stimulate a classroom discussion. Questions are a vital part of the Socratic method, but it's not so much about questioning people rather than lecturing to them.

At its heart, the Socratic method is about influence. A professor who asks questions without intent to influence isn't engaged in Socratic education. At best, such a professor involves everybody in the discussion, and everybody feels positive about what's going on in the classroom.

In a nutshell, Socrates never told people that they were wrong. Rather, he listened to their positions, asked questions, listened to the responses and asked more questions. His questions were very peculiar. First, most could be answered with one word, Yes. Second, his questions were designed to make people aware of the logical contradictions on which their arguments were founded. Socrates continued asking questions until his opponents found themselves agreeing to a position that they vehemently opposed only a few minutes earlier. Yet Socrates pulled them into agreement in a very rational, inoffensive way.

Socrates went to great lengths never to tell other people that they were wrong—even when he believed that they were. In fact, he usually led them to making this discovery on their own. His basic attitude was that the one thing he knew was "I can know nothing with absolute certainty." Here are some practical steps you can use to put the Socratic method to work:

- **Know your reasons and your interests.** Most people are familiar with the Socratic injunction, "Know thyself." Knowing yourself is the first step to using the Socratic method successfully. Specifically, you should know your values, your reasons and your interests. Socrates' mind was not empty. He had a very well developed worldview and system of thought. His positions gave him both a foundation for his own arguments and a yardstick that measured the power of his opponents' positions.

  In a business context, you may find it beneficial to frame your beliefs in terms of interests rather than positions. Here is an example. A buyer and a supplier, by definition, will work for different companies, and they would naturally approach their negotiating from opposing views as representatives of two unrelated companies. However, they could approach their negotiation in terms of shared interests. The obvious shared interest of all businesspeople is that they are focused on making a profit. This one shared interest provides a better foundation for building a mutually beneficial relationship than the differences between the two companies.

- **Assume you might be wrong.** Here's where humility comes in. Establish your own worldview, and then assume that you might be wrong on all or parts of it. Such an attitude prepares you to receive feedback and change more easily should you find yourself in error. People who never believe they are wrong find it difficult to change. Franklin tried to avoid absolute statements such as "It is obvious that . . ." and instead adopted more humble language like "I perceive that. . . ." A humble attitude helped him avoid causing defensiveness in his opponents. In addition, a willingness to assume you are wrong creates an environment in which others can more easily accept that they might be wrong, too.

- **Listen to the other person's position, and clarify your understanding with questions.** If the first necessity is being crystal clear in your interests and reasons, the second necessity is being crystal clear about the interests and reasons of the other party. In fact, whenever Socrates engaged in discussion, the other person did most of the talking early on. Socrates would listen carefully to what the other person had to say and then ask questions that probed and clarified that position.

Here's an example modified from an actual Socratic dialogue. John and his fellow manager, Thomas, are discussing the notion of fair pay in the workplace. Watch how John skillfully creates a listening environment and then carefully clarifies Thomas' ideas. You'll notice rather quickly that Thomas has a somewhat skewed notion of fairness.

John: Tell me, Thomas, what you think is fair and unfair pay. Once I know your ideas, then I will have a better understanding of how to evaluate paychecks, whether yours or somebody else's.

Thomas: I will tell you, if you're willing to listen.

John: I very much want to hear your ideas.

Thomas: Fairness, then, is when all workers get what they want, and unfairness is when they don't.

John: Very good, Thomas. You have now given me the sort of answer which we need to clarify these issues. But whether what you say is workable, I cannot as yet tell, although I have no doubt that you will prove the practicality of your ideas.

Thomas: Of course.

John: Well, then, let's take a closer look at some of our assumptions. When all workers get what they want, then that is fair. And when they don't get what they want, then that is un-fair. Did I understand you correctly?

Thomas: Yes, you did.

John: Would you agree that our payroll budget is limited by our company's resources?

Thomas: Yes, I would.

John: If I'm not mistaken, Thomas, there's never been a pay-day in our company when everybody in the company was paid the same amount. Do you think this is an accurate observation?

Thomas: I believe it is.

John: And further, Thomas, would you agree that there's a difference between the amount in somebody's paycheck and the process by which that amount is determined?

Thomas: Yes, I would agree to that, too.

John: So it's safe to assume that people in our company can be paid different amounts, and it can still be considered fair.

Thomas: So far, so good.

John: Tell me, Thomas, do you think we should simply ask people how much they want to be paid, or do you think we should have a different process for determining pay?

Thomas: Well, if you asked all workers how much they wanted, then we probably would not have enough money in the budget to cover it. I'd say we need a different process.

Note how John encourages Thomas to define his idea of fairness and expresses a willingness to hear Thomas' ideas (I very much want to hear your ideas). John should also be lauded for not balking when Thomas states his rather impossible concept of fairness. John listens to Thomas' definition and then repeats it to make sure he understands (Did I understand you correctly?). Also note that John tells Thomas that it will be Thomas who will eventually ". . . prove the practicality of his ideas."

After that, John starts to test Thomas' idea by asking questions that he can answer only in the positive (Yes I would, I believe it is). Through these questions, John gets Thomas to admit that budgets are limited, that people are used to having different rates of pay in the company, and that asking people how much they want to be paid is a bad idea. John has now laid a foundation to build a bridge between his and Thomas' ideas of fairness that Thomas will be willing to walk across.

● **Create a list of questions that build a bridge between your interests and the interests of the other person.** Nobody said this would be a brainless and effortless exercise! This is definitely the hard part and the place where the true Socratic masters earn their money. In the above example, John has a very different notion of fairness than Thomas'. However, he didn't immediately disagree with Thomas. Rather, he began the process of building a bridge between his ideas and Thomas' to test the truth of one or the other. Now John is well-positioned to get Thomas to accept the idea that the *process* of determining pay is much more central to the idea of fair pay than the actual result of how much everybody is paid. John knows that people are willing to live with what they perceive as unfair if they believe the *process* that determines those results is fair to everyone concerned.

Part of Socrates' genius was finding the common ground on which both parties could come to agreement. If we can assume that we're all in this together, then you and the other person must have complementary interests at some point. Questions are most persuasive when they compel the other person to take small steps away from his or her position while remaining aligned with his or her own interest.

How effective are Socratic-style methods of persuasion? Let the results speak for themselves in Franklin's own words:

"I found this Method safest for myself & very embarrassing to those against whom I used it, therefore I took a Delight in it, practis'd it continually & grew very artful & expert in drawing People even of superior Knowledge into Concessions the Consequences of which they did not foresee, entangling them in Difficulties out of which they could not extricate themselves, and so obtaining Victories that neither myself nor my Cause always deserved. I continu'd this Method some few years, but gradually left it, retaining only the Habit of expressing myself in Terms of modest Diffidence, never using when I advance any thing that may possibly be disputed, the Words, 'Certainly', 'undoubtedly', or any others that give the Air of Positiveness to

Still An Influence After All These Years

Dale Carnegie, author of the classic bestseller on personality development and influence, *How to Win Friends and Influence People*, learned his method by studying Benjamin Franklin. In his book, Carnegie praised Franklin for offering "some excellent suggestions about dealing with people and managing yourself and improving your personality . . . Benjamin Franklin's autobiography is one of the most fascinating life stories ever written, one of the classics of American literature. Borrow a copy from your public library or get a copy from your bookstore."

Franklin's legacy continues to amaze. He appears here as the centerpiece of one of the most significant self-help books ever written. In addition to the recommendation to read Franklin's autobiography, Carnegie shares a variety of stories from Franklin's life and some of his more memorable sayings. Through Carnegie's books and seminars alone, Franklin continues to be a key influence on 20th-century business practice.

an Opinion; but rather say, 'I conceive', or 'I apprehend' a thing to be so or so, 'It appears to me', or 'I should think it so or so for such & such Reasons', or 'I imagine it to be so', or 'it is so if I am not mistaken'. This Habit I believe has been of great Advantage to me, when I have had occasion to inculcate my Opinions & persuade men into Measures that I have been from time to time engag'd in promoting."

Franklin mastered the role of the humble but principal inquirer and found it more effective than forceful arguments for promoting his interests. Forceful arguments might yield a quick victory, but you'll most likely fail to create the influence with the other person that will serve you both better in the long run.

Love Your Enemies

Franklin promoted a rather peculiar attitude about how to handle enemies. His attitude is best captured in this quote from the 1756 edition of *Poor Richard's Almanac:* "Love your enemies, for they tell you your faults." You might think that Franklin peddled this advice solely because of the Puritan-centered Christian culture of the early American Colonies. However, Franklin by and large rejected the organized Christianity of his day and chose instead to worship at the altar of practicality. As such, he suggested loving your enemies because it might just be a practical and beneficial business maneuver.

How might the concept of loving your enemies be more beneficial than that of all-out war promoted by such business bestsellers as Sun Tzu's *The Art of War?* Let me offer several explanations:

- **It's hard to identify our true enemies.** I once heard that friends come and go, but enemies accumulate. So it's rather naive to promote the idea that everybody is a friend. Franklin believed that we all have enemies as well as friends. However, focusing all your energies on destroying your enemy can be bad policy. Apple Computer fell into this trap, which contributed to its rapid decline in the early 1990s.

  Throughout the 1980s Apple Computer targeted IBM as Corporate Enemy No. 1 and designed numerous ad campaigns that were aimed at destroying Big Blue (or was that Big Brother?). During the time Apple's energies were devoted to waging and winning the war against IBM, Microsoft was working furiously on the product that would all but consign Apple's Macintosh to the dustbin of the Digital Age. This product was a graphical user interface called Windows that would make the IBM PC and PC-compatible clones as easy to use as the Macintosh. Had Apple not misidentified its true enemy (or competitor), the history of the Digital Age might be very different indeed.

- **Not everyone is your enemy.** No name has left a more indelible mark on strategic thinking in the late 20th century than Michael Porter. Executives throughout America and the world studied his books, *Competitive Advantage* and *Competitive Strategy*. In fact, I still teach ideas from these two books in some of my business classes. Porter's insights into gaining and sustaining competitive advantage are great, but critics contend there's one big problem with his body of work: the word *competitive*. Isn't competition good? Yes, but not every company is your competitor. Advocates of the partnering school of thought have been quick to differentiate between companies with which you compete and those which are complementary.

When a business considers everyone to be its enemy (or competitor), then almost all business relationships end up as win-lose situations in which the key is to avoid being exploited by the other company. In contrast, an eye for complementary business activities results in creating mutually beneficial, win-win partnerships.

- **Your enemies have some good feedback for you.** The crux of Franklin's advice is that we should love our enemies primarily because they will often be the only ones who will tell us the truth about ourselves. We've all heard stories of managers who surround themselves with corporate "yes men" who do nothing more than affirm their managers' opinions and never challenge them. The stories exist because these dysfunctional managerial activities still occur.

Some managers are notorious for creating several reporting layers to insulate themselves from the front lines of business. The front-line workers—salespeople, customer service, hourly workers—

If Business Isn't War, Then What Is It?

suggest here that it's a bit dysfunctional to view business as war. However, if we can't describe it as war, then what exactly do we call it? In the spirit of political correctness I offer the following advice:

For years a few economists have argued that we need a new word to describe the marketplace. They argue that our business vocabulary is as outdated as "horseless carriage" to describe an automobile, and they propose the word "catallaxy." In 1838, Archbishop Whately first used it to describe the marketplace, and it has since been endorsed by economic giants like Ludwig von Mises and Friedrich Hayek.

"Catallaxy" is derived from the classical Greek word *katalattein*, which is roughly translated as "to exchange" in English. However, the word has some interesting baggage associated with it: *katalattein* also means "to receive into the community" and "to turn from enemy into friend." Advocates of this word believe that it more truly conveys the interaction of the marketplace where the goal is not to destroy or deceive another party but to find common interests that are mutually enriching.

Benjamin Franklin Once Said ...

"The wise Man draws more Advantage from his Enemies, than the Fool from his Friends."

Another way to think about the concept of competitive advantage is gaining an advantage *from* your competitors rather than *over* them. In fact, your competitive enemies can be your best teachers if your eyes are open to the lessons they teach. More than other teachers, our enemies will lead us to failure and show us our weaknesses. Success can be its own trap if managers quickly start to think that they are not only infallible but also invulnerable. Our enemies—our competitors—show us our weaknesses and give us the opportunity to either focus our businesses on other areas or improve our weaknesses and compete successfully.

Can you imagine the state of the U.S. automobile industry if German and Japanese cars had not been so popular in the 1970s and 1980s? U.S. manufacturers learned from their enemies that quality and fuel efficiency really did matter. I still remember cries to close the borders and stop foreign imports or the U.S. auto industry would never recover. Thankfully, those calls went unheeded, and U.S. auto manufacturers were forced to improve their products to win back their customers.

Our enemies help us focus our businesses by clearly showing us their strengths. Rather than risk engaging a competitor at their point of strength, we can differentiate ourselves and make our product or service more attractive to our shared customers. An example is the Cola Wars. Once Coke and Pepsi stopped trying to grab market share from each other and differentiated themselves as two distinct products, both companies found growing customer bases.

interact directly with the competitive environment and deal first-hand with the feedback from corporate "enemies," if you can consider an angry customer or supplier an enemy. Managers must establish ways of gathering feedback from people they would rather avoid, because these people may be telling you that they're about to go elsewhere with their money.

Little Favors Lead To Big Favors

When I was growing up, my favorite comic strip was *Dick Tracy*. Detective Tracy never failed to entertain me as he fought an array of interesting, almost grotesque, villains and narrowly escaped a menacing death trap at least once a month. He always took the opportunity to pass on bits of Tracy wisdom along the way, and one of my favorites was "Little crimes lead to big crimes." Tracy usually pointed this out when he busted a kid for a small crime and lovingly sent him to jail to teach him a lesson. Tracy figured that if he could save a few kids from a life of petty crime, he would ultimately save them from a life of bigger crimes.

Tracy's wisdom seems to cut both ways. Not only do small, negative events tend to lead to larger, negative events, but small, positive events have the potential of leading to larger, positive events. Franklin shares an interesting anecdote about such an occasion in his autobiography:

"It was about this time that . . . the Rev. Gilbert Tennet, came to me, with a Request that I would assist him in procuring a Subscription for erecting a new Meeting-house. It was to be for the Use of a Congregation he had gathered among the Presbyterians who were originally Disciples of Mr. Whitefield. Unwilling to make myself disagreeable to my fellow Citizens, by too frequently soliciting their Contributions, I absolutely refus'd. He then desir'd I would furnish him a List of the Names of Persons I knew by Experience to be generous and public-spirited. I thought it would be unbecoming in me, after their kind Compliance with my Solicitations, to make them out to be worried by other Beggars, and therefore refus'd also to give such a List. He then desir'd I would at least give him my Advice. That I will readily do, said I; and, in the first Place, I advise you to apply to all those whom you know will give something; next to those whom you are uncertain whether they will give any-thing or not; and show them the List of those who have given; and lastly, do not neglect those who you are sure will give nothing, for in some of them you may be mistaken. He laugh'd, thank'd me, and said he would take my Advice. He did so, for he ask'd of every body; and he obtain'd a much larger Sum than he expected, with which he erected the capacious and very elegant Meeting-house that stands in Arch Street."

Franklin was careful in this situation to safeguard not only his own reputation but also the well-being of the charitable individuals he knew in the community. He flatly refused both his time and his good name to help Tennet in raising funds for a new church building. In addition, Franklin was careful to protect those people from whom he had previously received funds so as to keep them from becoming fund-raising targets every time there was a new campaign to build a public project. Instead, Franklin showed Tennet how to begin his campaign by collecting first from the people that he was sure would give and then showing his list of contributors to other, less certain, contributors. Finally, only the humble Franklin would have advised asking those you don't think will give, because you just might be wrong about them.

Franklin shows us that using a simple but deliberate influence strategy can pay off handsomely. Modern research corroborates much of Franklin's advice in this situation. Most people are hesitant to promote campaigns for a public concern in a large way. For example, let's suppose that your community was holding an election to triple the fines on traffic violations for speeding in a school zone. When people were asked to display placards in their front yards promoting this cause, the vast majority declined. However, when the same people were asked to support the campaign in a smaller way—wearing a button or affixing a bumper sticker—they were more likely to agree. Further, when they were later approached to place placards in their yards, the acceptance rate on the second request was significantly higher.

How might these tactics work in business? Let's suppose you're trying to rally political support for a rather innovative project. It's a wild enough idea to cause a conservative backlash resulting in egg on your face. The common wisdom of "you scratch my back, and I'll scratch yours" is vastly different from these two influence tactics. First, rally support from your mentors and most trusted colleagues. Second, use this list of names to positively influence the skeptics in the crowd before formally airing the proposal. Finally, identify those who are undecided or potentially opposed and ask them for a small favor before the proposal is aired. Ask for something simple like retrieving a bit of budget information or dropping some papers off at someone else's desk. Although it can't guarantee their support, it will increase the odds of their doing you a bigger favor later on like supporting your new proposal.

Highbrow Or Lowbrow Influence?

If you want to influence people, then you have a very important choice to make. Will you influence a small number of elite players, or will you throw a wider net and influence a greater number of average citizens? Franklin chose to focus his influence efforts first on the typical Colonial citizen rather than the intellectual elite of his day. This was not because he couldn't speak the language of the elite, for he certainly could. Rather, he believed that the best base of influence was with the average citizen.

Other great American managers have followed Franklin's lead and marketed to the public at large rather than to more elite population segments. Henry Ford chose to democratize the automobile so that every American could own one rather than build luxury cars for smaller, elite markets. The result was his legendary Model T. Similarly, Sam Walton chose to cater to the vast majority of Americans who want better variety and lower prices. As a result, Wal-Mart was nobody's idea of a high-class shopping experience, but it became the dominant retailer of the late 20th century.

Although Franklin is a beloved figure in the minds of most Americans, he is thoroughly despised by the very highbrow intellectuals. This minority's views of Franklin are best captured in the comments of Charles Angoff, a little-known American literary historian who died in 1979. Here's a sample of comments on Franklin's autobiography from Angoff's book, *A Literary History of the American People*:

> "Franklin's most popular work was, and still is, his *Autobiography*. It was the longest of his writings, and the one he did most carelessly. He wrote it whenever he felt like it, and apparently cared very little if it was ever published. . . . His writings enjoyed a vast popularity in his own day, and still do in ours, but that should not blind us to their inferior quality. To call Franklin 'one of the greatest masters of English expression' is the veriest nonsense. But by his international prominence and

by the wide circulation of his two-penny philosophy he left a lasting impression on the national culture. In him the 'lowbrow' point of view for the first time took definite shape . . . and by the force of his personality did more than any other man in his day to graft it upon the American people. The vulgarity he spread is still with us."

Angoff was not alone in his highbrow, intellectual critique of Franklin's writings. Joining him are such notables as Mark Twain, creator of *Tom Sawyer* and *Huckleberry Finn*, and D.H. Lawrence, a 20th-century novelist you'll meet again in Chapter 7. Look at the words Angoff uses to describe Franklin: *two-penny, lowbrow, vulgar* and *popu-*

Pride: Not Your Average Deadly Sin

Franklin chose humility as a core value to guide his daily activities and decision making. You might think that pride would have been a better choice. Aren't people successful because they have the arrogance to think they know a better way? Donald Burr, former CEO of People Express Airlines, spoke via teleconference to one of my classes not long ago. People Express is one of the most amazing stories of success and failure in recent American business history. Its rapid rise and even more rapid decline continues to sell well as a Harvard Business School case study a decade later. During our conversation with Burr, a student asked if there was one thing Burr wished he had done differently. Burr replied: "I'd listen to my mother. She always said, 'Are you still listening?' " He then went on to describe how the rapid success of People Express resulted in pride and arrogance among its leaders, which caused them to stop listening to employees and customers, thinking they knew better. Burr suggested that this is a common temptation for people, like himself, who make the cover of *Time*, *Fortune* and dozens of other magazines. Burr claimed to have learned more from failure than from success, and the key lesson seemed to be that humility might be the cornerstone of success in a capitalist economy. Pride isn't one of the seven deadly sins for nothing.

lar. If I didn't know better, I'd say that Angoff is upset primarily because Franklin's work isn't intellectual enough.

In my opinion, this is precisely Franklin's genius. He's a household name, and Angoff is not, primarily because Franklin was and is accessible to the average American. Franklin secured his reputation early in his life with the creation of his annual *Poor Richard's Almanac.* People all across Colonial America purchased almanacs every year, as they were the calendars of the day. Almanacs contained charts calculating the changes of the moon and the tides in addition to a variety of poems, facts and sayings of various sorts. Through the fictional character Poor Richard, Franklin forever influenced American culture with sayings like "Early to bed and early to rise makes a man healthy, wealthy and wise."

Poor Richard's Almanac was not prestige literature; it was a business venture. The almanacs had to sell a lot of copies to be profitable, and Franklin's writing had to be witty enough and his counsel wise enough to ensure repeat customers year after year. Yet the very criticisms leveled upon Franklin from the academic elite are the reasons his influence remains to this day. He consciously chose to write for the largest audience possible. Beware of the temptation to sacrifice both influence and market power for the sake of appearing more intellectual or more prestigious. Franklin, Ford and Walton made the lowbrow choice—and it paid off handsomely.

What Good Shall I Do This Day?

❑ Adjust your thinking to view more people as partners rather than enemies. War and sports require enemies, but business requires partners.

❑ Seek to elicit more cooperation from everybody you meet. Try Axelrod's four guidelines: 1) Try cooperating the first time, 2) punish them if they fail to cooperate, 3) forgive them if they are willing to cooperate the next time, and 4) avoid deceptive strategies.

❑ Try to go the entire day without making an absolute statement like "without a doubt" or "certainly." Rather, learn to preface your ideas with "It appears to me . . ." or "If I am not mistaken . . ."

❑ Learn to be the humble inquirer rather than the forceful defender.

❑ Before engaging in a debate, make sure you understand your own interests.

❑ Build a bridge between your interests and the interests of the other party with a string of "yes" questions.

❑ Go to someone you've always considered an enemy, and listen to whatever feedback that person might have for you.

❑ Find somebody you've always considered an enemy, and discover common interests that will make that person a partner.

❑ Develop a more humble perspective about your opinions. You might just be wrong.

❑ Tailor your influence and message to cater to the broadest possible audience rather than please a few critics.

❑ Get other people to do small favors for you now, so they will do larger favors for you later on.

In short, the way to wealth, if you desire it, is as plain as the way to market. It depends chiefly on two words, industry and frugality; that is waste neither time nor money, but make the best use of both. Without industry and frugality nothing will do, and with them everything. He that gets all he can honestly, and saves all he gets (necessary expenses excepted), will certainly become rich, if that Being who governs the world, to whom all should look for a blessing on their honest endeavors, doth not, in his wise providence, otherwise determine.

—Benjamin Franklin
discussing the way to wealth in his
essay, *Advice to a Young Tradesman*

Chapter 5

Hard Work And Frugality: A Winning Combination

"**I** think I'm depressed."

Fritz is one of your firm's most essential workers and has one of the longest tenures with the company. Half an hour earlier, he had come into your office and shut the door. The two of you exchanged pleasantries, and then he launched into a long monologue expressing burnout and despair. Then he dropped the depression bomb on you and just sat waiting for your response.

You weren't expecting this, and you start flipping through various responses in your mind. "Trouble at home, Fritz?" No, that's too personal. "Fritz, what you need is a good anti-depressant." That's even worse. "Tell me about your childhood . . . ." Who do you think you are, Dr. Freud?

While you're frantically trying to think of something to say, Fritz continues. "I just can't seem to get anything done anymore. It seems like I'm running faster and faster and getting nowhere. I used to be a top performer, but the last couple of years I've been slipping. I'm so unsatisfied here. Maybe it's time for me to move on to something else."

You certainly don't want to lose Fritz and his expertise, but he is right about his performance. You've noticed him slipping the last few years. What can you do to help him?

Make Them Scour The Anchor: Franklin On Job Satisfaction

Job satisfaction is widely believed to be important in the workplace. Employee satisfaction is believed to affect productivity, absenteeism, collegiality, and the thousand and one supportive behaviors that all good corporate citizens must contribute outside their particular job roles to keep an organization functioning. If job satisfaction is so important, what exactly is its relationship to employee productivity, and should managers make job satisfaction a workplace priority? Franklin had definite opinions about whether managers should worry about worker morale and productivity, which are captured in his next management principle.

Franklin's Fifth Rule Of Management: Work hard and watch your costs.

In 1755, the British sent English troops to the American colonies to quell some disturbances that had the potential to turn into war with the French. Franklin was put in charge of a military company to advance and defend the northwestern frontier in Pennsylvania from any attacker, French or otherwise. The defense was undertaken primarily by organizing militia companies and building forts.

Franklin made some important observations about human behavior during this military campaign. He writes:

"This gave me the occasion to observe, that when Men are employ'd they are best contented. For on the Days they work'd they were good-natur'd and cheerful; and with the consciousness of having done a good Day's work they spent the Evenings jollily; but on the idle Days they were mutinous and quarrelsome, finding fault with their Pork, the Bread, etc. and in continual ill-humor; which put me in mind of a Sea-Captain whose Rule it was to keep his Men constantly at Work; and when his Mate once told him that they had done every thing, and there was nothing farther to employ them about; 'O,' says he, 'make them scour the Anchor.'"

Franklin shares some interesting conclusions about workplace attitudes in this passage. How does a manager keep employees good-natured and cheerful as opposed to being quarrelsome and continually in poor humor? In essence, Franklin advises managers to manage for productivity rather than satisfaction.

The relationship between productivity and satisfaction can be analyzed from two perspectives. First, we could hypothesize that happy (satisfied) workers are productive workers. In contrast, we could argue that productive workers are satisfied workers.

Each perspective seems equally plausible, and an experienced manager could probably marshal anecdotal evidence to support either proposition. Franklin's observations clearly point to the latter, but skeptics might argue that we now live in a more enlightened age, and we must understand the human psyche. Fortunately, a great deal of systematic study in the behavioral sciences has addressed this relationship.

In the mid-1970s, Dr. Edwin Locke, a behavioral scientist at the University of Maryland, published a definitive statement about whether job satisfaction leads to higher productivity or vice versa. Before publishing his conclusions, Locke read more than 3,000 studies that dealt with the relationship between job satisfaction and on-the-job productivity. He concluded and successfully argued that job satisfaction has no direct effect on employee productivity. Rather, the scientific evidence from systematic, controlled observations suggests that higher productivity results in job satisfaction and not the reverse. In other words, Franklin's casual observations have been confirmed by behavioral scientists more than 200 years later. Emotions and attitudes may matter in the workplace, but they do not seem to be the key that unlocks worker productivity.

Dr. Locke's systematic research goes further than Franklin's casual observations, however. Locke concluded that higher productivity leads to increased job satisfaction only in cases in which higher productivity results in job performance that is important to the individual employee. In other words, it's unlikely that the modern-day equivalent of "making them scour the anchor" would result in greater job satisfaction. Work simply for the sake of work will not lead to higher levels of job satisfaction among employees. Rather, higher productivity and positive workplace attitudes will result if the work projects are valued by the individual employee. Franklin's prescription for industry, or hard work, is still good medicine for curing the emotional ills of the modern workplace.

Industry And Frugality In Today's Marketplace

Franklin's simple admonition to work hard and watch your costs has been a recipe for success since the days of Colonial America. Hard-working employees are not only more satisfied and emotionally healthy, but they contribute a great deal of revenue to the bottom line. Franklin's concepts of industry and frugality were at the center of two great retailing stories of the 20th century.

Ben Franklin stores were one of the first great chains of variety stores that swept across America in the years between World War I and World War II. Variety stores attempted to carry a wider array of goods than their more focused competitors like auto-supply stores. Further, variety stores aimed at serving consumers abandoned by more upscale retailers like Marshall Field's. The Butler brothers of Chicago, who had been merchants since 1887, started Ben Franklin stores in 1920. They chose the Ben Franklin name because it represented thrift and honesty, which they hoped would attract customers. Additionally, the Franklin name was just good currency.

Sam Walton opened his first Ben Franklin store in 1945 and increased the number of Walton-managed Ben Franklin franchises to 15 by the end of the 1950s. In 1962, Walton proposed to the top executives at Ben Franklin that they consider moving into a new, but as yet untested, development in retailing—the discount store. The proposal did not fly with the executives at Ben Franklin primarily because their profit margin would have been cut on the wholesale merchandise they sold to their franchise retailers. Why go from making a comfortable 20 percent to 25 percent profit margin in variety-store retailing and start making between 10 percent and 15 percent in discount-store retailing? Fat profit margins meant a more comfortable lifestyle for those managers.

Unfortunately for Ben Franklin stores, the company was about to be trumped by a businessman who was more hard-working and more frugal. In fact, Sam Walton may have been even more hard-working and more frugal than Benjamin Franklin himself. After being rejected by the Ben Franklin executives, Sam Walton went on, at age 44, to establish the first Wal-Mart. His vision of discount retailing with lower margins and higher volume would dominate American retailing and squeeze the five-and-dime variety store—like the Ben Franklin chain—out of business.

Try to think of industry (hard work) and frugality as principles guiding revenue generation and cost reduction, respectively. Franklin's ideas about hard work can build a firm's revenues. Likewise, his ideas about frugality can help control costs. Hard work without frugality is potentially dangerous, however. Adopting the principle of frugality alone might lead you to think that you can save your way to prosperity. This is simply not true. In contrast, adopting only the principle of hard work might result in growth being eaten up by excess costs of labor or communication. A commitment to both principles will provide a healthy balance for your business.

Being Industrious In The Post-Industrial Age

We all carry mental images of what it means to work hard. I grew up working in cotton fields and warehouses, and my image of hard work is hoeing weeds out of a cotton field in the blazing west Texas summer sun. Another image I have is unloading crate after crate of Phillips 66 oil products from an 18-wheeler and stacking them up to a 12-foot ceiling—without the use of a forklift. For centuries, this type of hard, physical labor constituted the idea of real work.

The closest most of us get to this kind of hard, physical labor is mowing our lawns or pushing our cars down the freeway when we run out of gas. This is not to say that physical work no longer exists, for it most certainly does. Agricultural and warehouse workers comprise significant segments of the American labor force. However, if you're a manager, you probably gave up this type of work when you first took on a managerial role. Further, even most nonmanagerial jobs in the post-industrial world are sedentary and nonphysical.

We are left, then, with a peculiar predicament: If we seek to be as industrious as Benjamin Franklin, how do we know when we're doing so if the nature of work has changed so dramatically? We could score ourselves by the number of hours we work each week, but this practice might not really encourage us to work more effectively. Here are some ways managers and workers can measure hard work in the Digital Age.

- **Growth of a personal network:** Now more than ever, *who you know* is more important than *what you know*. One of the best performance goals for your next round of performance evaluations is requiring employees to increase the size of their Rolodexes and electronic address books by 20 percent. Meeting new people is intense, difficult work. Most of us would rather sit in our quiet offices and avoid the trouble of remembering names and sharing clever conversation.

  The old networks were exclusive and club-centered, but the new networking opportunities are more inclusive. The old Four C's— college, civic organizations, church and country club—may still be important, but good networking now demands more. The new Four C's appear to be chat rooms, coffee bars, community volunteering and commuter networking in planes, trains and carpools.

- **Intensity of personal communications:** In Franklin's day, communication occurred only through personal visits and hand-written, hand-delivered letters. Communication changed little until the invention of the telegraph and telephone in the 1800s. Since then, a revolution in communication technology has occurred. We now have more media and more communication channels than ever before, and this revolution in communication technology may have fueled the worldwide growth in free markets. Markets are created when two parties exchange products or services, and exchange occurs *only* when two parties communicate with each other.

  Currently, hard work is happening whenever people are talking on cell phones or auctioning goods on the Internet. A willingness to

Benjamin Franklin Once Said . . .

"He that waits upon Fortune, is never sure of a Dinner."

Making luck the centerpiece of your firm's strategy is one of the worst things you can do, according to Franklin. Luck-centered people sit around all day hoping to be lucky enough to have customers come to them. Such strategies remind me of the dozens of vendors in stationary carts at Tiananmen Square in Beijing, all hoping to be lucky enough that the next tour bus will stop by their cart. Some people who go out of business justify it by claiming that they are unlucky.

Another popular luck-based strategy is waiting for your lucky break. We've all heard stories of movie stars plucked from the crowd while waiting tables or shopping for groceries. And what about the bingo parlor? Bingo is a game of probabilities, yet many players believe that bringing items like statues or stuffed animals and arranging them in certain ways will increase their odds of winning. Most likely, if they are winning, it's because they have played bingo so long that they have developed complex rituals.

Even if business is just a game of probabilities, then hard work and frugality are about increasing the probabilities of success. People who are working hard and watching their costs are more likely to create opportunity for themselves than people who sit around waiting for their lucky break. Condemning luck as a strategic imperative is not to say that luck never plays a part in business success. It most certainly does. History is full of companies that were in the right place at the right time. However, these so-called lucky firms were usually busy pursuing their goals when they stumbled across their gold mine. They certainly were not sitting around waiting for something good to happen.

connect should be considered a selection criterion for every new employee. Management guru Tom Peters captures this new communication intensity: He who makes the most phone calls wins. The game may be won or lost on the cell phones you should be providing to all employees who need them.

- **Speed of response:** One good measure of hard work in the Digital Age is how quickly problems get solved or how quickly new ideas get turned into marketable products and services. The current wisdom in Silicon Valley is that one year of work in an Internet-based firm is equivalent to six years of work in a traditional organization because workers in Internet-based firms work longer hours, create more services and explore more frontiers in a year than other workers do in six years.

The new industriousness is not just about going farther but getting there faster. It means jumping on an airplane on short notice to handle a problem with important clients or customers. It means writing code for three days straight to make sure everything is just right for a new product launch. It means increasing market demand with a working prototype rather than waiting for a finished product to be developed.

- **Number of successful failures:** A successful failure? Such a beast can exist. A failure is successful if it provides you with feedback so rich that it results in a new business opportunity. New Coke is an example. It provided the Coca-Cola Co. with the strategic focus they needed to become the dominant force they have been throughout the 1990s.

The new industriousness is about not punishing failure. College is not a good training ground for new managers because students are socialized to avoid failure at all costs. Managers must train new failure-avoiding employees to fail and to learn from their failures. If you're worried about failure overtaking the organization, then demand that every failure be accounted for in related products or services. Successful failures will not occur when workers fail and then run off to lick their wounds in unrelated projects.

- **Frequency of new experiences:** I lived in Texas during the first 30 years of my life and then moved to California for two years during the late 1990s. During my time in California, I had many "vuja daze" experiences. While *déjà vu* occurs when you realize that you have experienced the moment you are currently experiencing before, "vuja daze" is just the opposite both phonetically and literally. "Vuja daze" occurs when you suddenly realize that you are experiencing something you have *never* experienced before. When you live in small Texas towns most of your life and then move to California, you experience a great deal of "vuja daze."

The new industriousness suggests that routine has the potential to be a competitive trap. How often are you experiencing something totally different from your daily routine? The new concept of hard work demands a commitment to intense, new experiences. Try living one morning each month with one of your firm's typical customers. Do you offer products or services to mothers of preschoolers? If so, instead of paying some market research firm to conduct a focus group, shed the business suit and spend a morning with a mom and her toddlers. Looking to do business in China? Get out of your middle-class American rut and start watching Chinese language films, or go to the closest Chinatown and hang out in the street for a bit before going in the restaurant. Better yet, go directly to China and start making some Chinese friends around the turntable at the restaurant of their choice.

The Bald Eagle: A National Bad Example

Franklin adamantly opposed the adoption of the bald eagle as the national symbol of the new United States of America. He wrote in a letter to a friend that the bald eagle was a ". . . Bird of bad moral Character; he does not get his living honestly; you may have seen him perch'd on some dead Tree, near the River where, too lazy to fish for himself, he watches the Labour of the Fishing-Hawk; and, when that diligent Bird has at length taken a Fish, and is bearing it to his Nest for the support of his Mate and young ones, the Bald Eagle pursues him, and takes it from him."[*]

Franklin despised using the bald eagle as our national symbol primarily because of its inherent lack of hard work. He compared the bald eagle to men who make their living as thieves and robbers and condemned the society that is populated solely by such "workers." Franklin's own choice for our national symbol was the turkey, which he preferred because it was native to North America.

[*]*Source:* The Autobiography And Other Writings *(Penguin Classics)*

Working Hard Or Just Busy?

There's a big difference between working hard and being busy. To me, hard working suggests that your activities are accomplishing important goals. In the absence of a guiding plan for your life, hard work can easily digress into unfocused busywork. Consider once again Franklin's example for guidance on this point. Franklin set the stan-

Benjamin Franklin Once Said ...

"The favour of the Great is no inheritance."

Benjamin Franklin had a great deal to say in his autobiography about how to acquire wealth and achieve success. Likewise, he had a great deal to say about how to ensure the lack of wealth. One sure way to increase the odds of failing is to rely on the promises of those with nothing to offer but, well . . . promises.

Franklin learned this lesson the hard way early in his life when a high-ranking political figure who was liberal with promises persuaded young Franklin to set up his own print shop. Franklin naively agreed to board a ship for London to purchase his supplies, and the politician promised to send numerous letters of credit and reference with Franklin when the ship sailed. Needless to say, the ship sailed and arrived in London, and no letters were ever found from the politician. Franklin was left to his own wits to make his way in London a bit wiser to hollow political promises. Franklin characterized the man as wanting to please everybody and, having nothing to give, ". . . he gave expectations."

The best plan for the future is to rely most heavily on the factors that you can influence. You can do very little to make another's promise a genuine reality. You can, however, work hard, watch your costs and persevere in creating opportunity for yourself and your company.

dard for making good use of a trip across the Atlantic. After returning from London, Franklin had this to say about his activities during the two-and-a-half-month crossing:

> "For the Incidents of the Voyage, I refer you to my Journal, where you will find them all minutely related. Perhaps the most important Part of that Journal is the Plan to be found in it which I formed at Sea, for regulating my future Conduct in Life. It is the more remarkable, as being form'd when I was so young, and yet being pretty faithfully adhered to quite thro' to old Age."

First, let's be thankful that we travel from England to America in less than a day instead of two and a half months. Second, let's marvel at Franklin's clarity of vision in developing a plan to guide his life's activities at only 22 years of age. Without hesitation, I will say that the turbulence and changing opportunities of our modern environment make the development of a five-year plan difficult and a Franklinesque 65-year plan virtually impossible. Still, the basic principle rings true. Even if it has to be revised annually, a plan for your own life and your business will probably make the difference between forward momentum and wasteful busywork.

The New Frugality

Just as the nature of hard work has changed during the past 200 years, so has the nature of frugality. Franklin's ideas about frugality are important to today's managers, but they need a little work to bring them successfully into the modern context. For example, one of Franklin's favorite frugal practices was going to bed without an evening meal. The way he figured it, you not only saved the cost of the meal, but because you were asleep, you were oblivious to experiencing hunger. Although the exercise might have a lesson or two in it, it really isn't practical management advice for today's managers. Here are some examples of what it means to be frugal in the Digital Age.

- **Use appropriate technologies.** Finding the right balance of technology and utility to best meet your competitive demands is challenging. Some technologies are so advanced that they miss out on the possibility of becoming industry standards. Steve Jobs' NeXT computer is a great example of a technology that was too advanced for its day and failed to be adopted by consumers. In contrast, everybody is aware how quickly some technologies become outdated. Trying to compete with outdated manufacturing, communication or information technologies is like bringing a knife to a gunfight—it just won't help you much.

I'll talk about outdated technologies in the last chapter, so let's focus here on new technologies. New technologies can be classified into two equally dangerous categories: seductive and unproven. Seductive technologies are mainstream technologies that have been proven to be genuinely handy in certain situations. Two good examples are cell phones and laptop computers, both of which are more expensive than their conventional counterparts, the ground-wire telephone and the desktop computer. However, the expense is offset by the freedom afforded to users. As good as this technology is, think of the disruption if *everybody* in your firm had cell phones and laptops for all their work. Good things might happen, but you could end up paying a premium price for the phones and computers that many people just kept on their desks. The new frugality demands seeking technological appropriateness and avoiding seductive technologies just because they seem . . . well, seductively cool.

● **Keep discretionary costs under control.** A firm's costs are either predictable or discretionary. Predictable costs, such as payroll, can be easily forecast from past data. Your payroll costs for the coming quarter can be easily predicted if you know your head count and production targets. Discretionary costs, on the other hand, such as advertising, are just the opposite. Past budgets can show how much you spent, but very few companies can really establish meaningful relationships between money spent on advertising and increases in sales. It clearly happens, but it's difficult to quantify how much sales revenue results per advertising dollar spent.

One of the best ways to keep discretionary costs—such as advertising—under control is through benchmarking against the averages of other firms. A group of companies can hire a consulting firm or trade association to consolidate their averages in a document such as the *Value of Advertising* compiled by the American Association of Advertising Agencies (AAAA).

The AAAA collects multiyear budgetary information from companies to improve both the process of setting an advertising budget and the creation of credible measurements of advertising performance. Basically, companies turn over their advertising and sales budgets to the AAAA, which then consolidates these figures with their existing database and gives the results back to the participating companies. By using the AAAA, companies can remain anonymous to competitors and still receive valuable feedback on their advertising practices. Without the numbers you get from benchmarking, you're like a pilot flying without an instrument panel. You may be spending more money than necessary to solve your advertising challenges.

Benjamin Franklin Once Said ...

"When 'tis fair be sure to take your Great coat with you."

Frugality may well be the best disaster insurance in which you could ever invest. Franklin suggests in this quote that business and life are cyclical in nature. Just as the weather cycles from dry to rainy, business activity can cycle from extremely busy to extremely slow. Franklin warns us not to be overconfident during the busy times. Rather, he recommends using the good times to prepare for the storm that is certain to come someday.

This viewpoint is quite different from how most people run their businesses and personal lives. At the first sign of prosperity, many of us start spending our newly acquired surplus money on "wish list" items, such as personal objects or new furnishings for the office. Franklin's attitude of always preparing for the storm resulted in his being a self-financing businessman. He was a creditor for most of his life, lending money to others. In contrast, most of us are debtors, always taking out loans to finance our dreams. Let Franklin's example be a lesson to you: Prepare for the worst by always watching your costs, and should you avoid the worst, you'll be well positioned for the future.

- **Eliminate nonvalue-added activities.** A revolution in cost accounting in the past decade has resulted in many businesses dividing their efforts into two lists: value-added and nonvalue-added activities. Value-added activities produce clear and quantifiable revenue growth or cost reductions. In contrast, nonvalue-added activities do not.

  Managers have removed unnecessary or redundant steps in the manufacturing process, reduced the number of reports required by workers and eliminated unnecessary (but longstanding) meetings and committees. Some travel-related businesses have gotten rid of fancier-than-necessary hotel rooms and unnecessary gadgets in rental cars. Some people criticize this movement as resulting in too many no-frills products and services, but most agree that it has given consumers more value for their money. The new frugality demands that every activity in your business makes a contribution to the bottom line—or it gets eliminated.

- **Use just-in-time inventory control.** Sure, everybody's heard this buzzword, but few really recognize its true power. Inventory eats up enormous amounts of cash in businesses. Most of our inventory habits evolved from the time when transportation and communication were less reliable, when it was smart to stockpile additional inventory. These days, such stockpiling is much more risky.

  The most competitive businesses today keep shockingly low levels of inventory. I toured a manufacturing facility not long ago in which the parts were delivered in trucks on one side of the plant, were assembled into products as they moved through the plant, and left in trucks as finished products on the other side of the plant. In other words, the plant was for assembly rather than storage. Almost nothing was left in the parts bins or on the floor at the end of the shift. Such a level of inventory control has allowed the company to break all kinds of records because cash isn't tied up in inventory or obsolete parts and products when innovations occur.

- **Practice Spartan-style management.** The Spartans were ancient Greek warriors who spurned luxury and indulgence during wartime for the promise of better soldiers. When other troops feasted nightly and lived in luxurious tents attended by dozens of servants, the Spartans were sleeping outdoors and living off a subsistence diet. Just for the record, the Spartans won a lot of their battles.

Spartan-style managers have a skeptical attitude toward unnecessary luxuries. When every dollar counts during the start-up phase of a business, a Spartan-style manager will settle for good, used office furniture rather than buy high-end, new furniture. Unnecessary luxuries in the workplace are tempting, but they ultimately affect your own bottom line. Here are a few phrases you would never hear from a Spartan-style manager:

1. "It's good company policy to send everything by overnight delivery."

2. "Let's fly first class again."

3. "Sure, we'll have another round of dessert. It's on the company card."

4. "I'd like a nicer hotel, please, and make sure that rental car is a convertible."

5. "Can't we find thicker carpet for our offices?"

Sam's Gone, What Now?

Sam Walton succumbed to cancer in 1992, leaving his beloved company in somebody else's hands. Walton was the kind of founder—like Walt Disney or Herb Kelleher of Southwest Airlines—who leaves an indelible cultural imprint on a company. When strong founders like these men pass away, however, their cultural legacy starts to dissipate.

Sam Walton created a culture of frugality at Wal-Mart. Employees shared hotel rooms and taxis when they traveled on company business. Everybody paid for their own coffee at the office. Sam Walton, the richest man in America in his day, bought his own suits at Wal-Mart. Now, eight years after his death, are his employees still as frugal? History suggests that frugality wanes after a founder dies, as success brings the temptation of luxury. So far, however, Walton's torch of frugality has been passed to the next generation of managers at Wal-Mart. Time will tell if Sam Walton's Wal-Mart can avoid the temptation of luxury and continue to succeed where the Ben Franklin variety stores failed.

How Leisure And Luxury
Creep Up On You

If hard work and frugality have opposite concepts, they are leisure and luxury. Franklin was acutely aware of how easily leisure activities and luxurious costs could creep up. He wrote about the turning point in his own household when leisure and luxury first appeared after years of hard work and frugality:

"We kept no idle Servants, our Table was plain & simple, our Furniture of the cheapest. For instance my Breakfast was a long time Bread & Milk, (no Tea) and I ate it out of a two penny earthen Porringer with a Pewter Spoon. But mark how Luxury will enter Families, and make a Progress, in Spite of Principle. Being call'd one Morning to Breakfast, I found it in a China Bowl with a Spoon of Silver. They had been bought for me without my Knowledge by my Wife, and had cost her the enormous Sum of three and twenty Shillings, for which she had no other Excuse or Apology to make, but that she thought her Husband deserved a Silver Spoon & China Bowl as well as any of his Neighbors."

Most businesses begin with a commitment to hard work and frugality more out of competitive necessity than personal principle. You can barely make payroll each month, but if you work hard enough and cut a few corners, then you can just get by. Franklin wisely notes that if you "just get by" for long enough and actually start to prosper, then the temptation toward leisure and luxury will appear. "Neighbors" who parade their luxurious goods before you hinting that you, too, deserve to live a little worsen the pressure. When this temptation comes, remember Franklin's advice to the young tradesmen of his day, which still may be your best operating principle: The fastest way to prosperity is still to work hard and watch your costs.

What Good Shall I Do This Day?

☐ Manage for productivity rather than satisfaction. Hard work can cure a variety of workplace ills.

☐ Experience "vuja daze" by intentionally seeking out an experience you've never had before.

☐ Add a new name to your address book—written or electronic.

☐ Send the signal that failure is appropriate in your organization. Consider making heroes of workers who fail, learn from the experience and then succeed on a related project.

☐ Stay connected with your most important people. It's easier than ever before. Don't send hand-written notes though; call them on your cell phone.

☐ Remember the bald eagle. Exalt hard-working employees in the workplace over those who live a life of leisure and survive by preying on others.

☐ Start monitoring response times on all important activities. Next, create ways to reduce response time and increase speed to market.

☐ Develop a plan to guide activities, or you'll be busy instead of industrious. If you can plan only for one day, that's a good start.

☐ Choose appropriate technologies whenever possible. Technology can leverage productivity, but it can also be a money pit.

☐ Eliminate waste by eliminating activities and resources that don't add value to your bottom line.

☐ Free up cash and eliminate waste by keeping your inventory under control.

☐ Consider benchmarking yourself against peers and industry averages when keeping discretionary costs under control.

☐ Even if you master your costs, keep an eye on them. Luxury and leisure have a way of creeping up on you.

I believe I have omitted mentioning that in my first Voyage from Boston, being becalm'd off Block Island, our People sat about catching Cod & haul'd up a great many. Hitherto I had stuck to my Resolution of not eating animal Food; and on this Occasion, I consider'd with my Master Tryon, the taking every Fish as a kind of unprovok'd Murder, since none of them had or ever could do us any Injury that might justify the Slaughter. All this seem'd very reasonable. But I had formerly been a great Lover of Fish, & when this came hot out of the Frying Pan, it smelled admirably well. I balanc'd some time between Principle & Inclination; till I recollected, that when the Fish were opened, I saw smaller Fish taken out of their Stomachs: Then thought I, if you eat one another, I don't see why we mayn't eat you. So I din'd upon Cod very heartily and continu'd to eat with other People, returning only now & then occasionally to a vegetable Diet. So convenient a thing it is to be a reasonable Creature, since it enables one to find or make a Reason for every thing one has a mind to do.

—Benjamin Franklin
on the reason why he
broke his vegetarian diet

Chapter 6

Let Reason
Work For You

"**S**o, what's your recommendation?"

You always hate that question during a presentation. It seems like it's one of those questions that you can never answer correctly. You feel quite passionate about the direction in which the company should be heading. You're just not sure whether your superiors feel the same. You know that the company needs to change direction in the next year or two because its current customer base is eroding. Somebody's going to have to pull a rabbit out of a hat, and you hope to be the one to do it.

You've waited as long as possible to respond, and the moment of truth arrives. You look across the table, and say in your firmest voice, "I feel like we should . . ."

A Reasonable Approach
To Presenting New Ideas

Benjamin Franklin might have some advice for you at this point in your presentation. Let's look again at the closing sentence in the quotation on page 84: "So convenient a thing it is to be a reasonable Creature, since it enables one to find or make a Reason for every thing one has a mind to do." This one sentence from the autobiography speaks volumes about Franklin's effectiveness in persuading others to accept new ideas. Central to his approach was the power of *reason* in making recommended actions acceptable to others. Further, Franklin advises us "to find or make a reason" to justify a course of action. He suggests that we must be creative in putting forward our reasons for our recommendations.

Here's how this approach might apply to the presentation scenario. Franklin would first advise avoiding the word "feel" in your response and in your own thinking. He would probably say that feeling is an emotional response to the problem, but "reason" is a more intellectual approach. Passion might help you make a more interesting presentation, but it shouldn't be the only thing you have to offer. Additionally, while feeling is a personal evaluation, reason is a broader-based approach that moves the debate into the arena of facts and market reality, away from your personal domain. In other words, stop feeling and start reasoning.

Franklin's second piece of advice would be to create reasonable justifications for your recommended courses of action. Most likely, your superiors need ideas, or they wouldn't be listening to presentations. Franklin would recommend building your presentation around a logical, central argument and using as many available facts as possible to support your ideas.

For example, let's suppose that you believe your company should start building a base of customers aged 20 to 30. First, you should collect as much data as possible about this market segment. A second idea might be to put together some cost and revenue projections for reaching this market. Finally, think about building into your presentation the argument that it might be a bad idea to base the future of the company on a different demographic segment such as middle-aged professionals or retired people.

Thus, Franklin might suggest responding with something like, "I think the company's future is with the 20-something market. Let me show you some market research and budget projections. . . ." In other words, Franklin would recommend that you create the reason your superiors need to accept your ideas.

Franklin's Sixth Rule Of Management:
Everybody wants to appear reasonable.

Benjamin Franklin was a child of the Enlightenment, and this fact would significantly shape his managerial actions. The Enlightenment was a period of intellectual awakening that occurred during the 50 years before Franklin's birth in 1706. The philosophy of the Enlightenment stressed that human activity should be guided by reason rather than by the mysticism and superstition that predominated during the Middle Ages. As a result of the influence of the Enlightenment, Benjamin Franklin understood something very basic about human nature: Almost everybody wants to appear reasonable. That is, he believed that we want others to think we're guided by reason rather than custom and superstition.

Franklin is well-known for putting the power of reason to work in his scientific activities such as his famous electricity experiment with the kite. However, Franklin also leveraged the power of reason to solve performance problems in the workplace. He did so by challenging people to consider the reasonableness of their working habits.

Drink Your Way To
Higher Productivity

Franklin's autobiography recounts an incident in which he used the power of reason to challenge some fellow workers who stubbornly clung to their customary belief that drinking beer at work made them more productive. This confrontation occurred during the period in his life when he worked as a journeyman in a printing house in London.

"At my first Admission into this Printing House, I took to working at the Press, imagining I felt a Want of the Bodily Exercise

I had been us'd to in America, where Presswork is mix'd with Composing. I drank only Water; the other Workmen, near 50 in Number, were great Guzzlers of Beer. On occasion I carried up & down Stairs a large Form of Types in each hand, when others carried but one in both Hands. They wonder'd to see from this & several Instances that the water-American as they call'd me was stronger than themselves who drank strong Beer. We had an Ale-house Boy who attended always in the House to supply the Workmen. My Companion at the Press, drank every day a Pint before Breakfast, a Pint at Breakfast with his Bread and Cheese; a Pint between Breakfast and Dinner; a Pint at Dinner; a Pint in the Afternoon about Six o'Clock, and another when he had done his Day's-Work. I thought it a detestable Custom. But it was necessary, he suppos'd, to drink strong Beer that he might be strong to labor."

Franklin was dealing here with a case of bad theory circulating among his fellow workers. Apparently, their theory of productivity was that strong beer resulted in strong labor. Although their exact reasons remain unclear, Franklin later suggested that they were under the impression that the wheat used in making the beer they drank provided nutrients for improving their work output.

In all fairness, there is some legitimacy to this theory considering that the incident occurred in England two centuries before the mass production of beer. British beer is notoriously strong to the average American's palate, in contrast to the rather bland, watery, mass-produced American beers. This beer was probably closer to liquid bread. Franklin, however, put to rest the reasonableness of this theory with a simple, reasonable theory of his own.

"I endeavor'd to convince him that the Bodily Strength afforded by Beer could only be in proportion to the Grain or Flour of the Barley dissolved in the Water of which it was made; that there was more Flour in a Penny-worth of Bread, and therefore if he would eat that with a Pint of Water, it would give him more Strength than a Quart of Beer. He drank on however, & had 4 or 5 Shillings to pay out of his Wages every Saturday Night for that Muddling Liquor; an Expense I was free from. And thus these poor Devils keep themselves always under."

It's important to note that the first tool that Franklin reached for to analyze his workplace problems was a reasonable theory to explain

Benjamin Franklin Once Said . . .

"God heals, and the Doctor takes the Fees."

In this saying, Franklin gives us plenty to think about the next time we consider hiring an external consultant to solve a problem. Have you priced a consultant lately to come into your organization and solve a problem like employee morale or low productivity? Most charge outrageous fees! Franklin challenges us here to consider the possibility that a system might just heal itself if given enough time.

Franklin understood that variability in performance is a fact of life. In other words, what goes up must come down and vice versa. Therefore, the next time your firm takes a downturn, you should be very careful before you hire an external consultant to fix the problem. The very real possibility exists that performance will eventually improve without intervention, and you could save a hefty consultant's fee.

In the future, consider a few medical guidelines when debating whether to hire a consultant for your firm. First, is this an emergency? If your problem is a sudden drop rather than a slow decline, then maybe a trip to the consultant's emergency room is justifiable. Second, is there a clear diagnosis? Vague illnesses at the doctor's office lead to vague and often overly expensive medications and tests. The more clearly the problem can be labeled ahead of time, the more successful and justifiable an intervention might be. Finally, is this a lingering illness? If the performance downturn is significantly beyond anything the company has previously experienced, then maybe it's time to get some help for this "lingering cough." You might find that it's symptomatic of a more serious health problem that nobody at your firm recognizes. In the end, a little caution when using consultants might save a great deal of money.

A Reason To Invest

Berkshire Hathaway is one of the greatest success stories in American business history. Berkshire Hathaway is a holding company in Omaha, Nebraska, that is run by legendary manager and investment guru Warren Buffet. Over the course of the past 15 years, Berkshire Hathaway's financial performance has left market-indexed mutual funds in the dust.

Warren Buffet is responsible for all the investment decisions at Berkshire Hathaway. Although Buffet hasn't written a book about his investment principles, his annual letters to shareholders have become required reading in investment circles. Buffet has never explicitly stated his decision-making rules and investment strategies. However, one thing is very, very clear: Buffet never invests in a new stock unless he has a powerful reason to do so. He doesn't invest on a hunch. He doesn't invest on a hot tip. And he certainly doesn't invest based on anybody's forecast of the future. He invests only in companies that he understands and has reason to believe are seriously undervalued. Reason has paid big dividends to Buffet and his shareholders.

workplace occurrences. Put simply, Franklin argued that nutrition indeed affected workplace productivity and that more nutrition was available in a loaf of bread than a quart of beer. By making his fellow workers aware of this simple, reasonable argument, Franklin was leveraging the idea that people will choose to appear reasonable when forced to choose between superstition and reason.

AA The Franklin Way

Franklin ultimately changed the behavior patterns of his overindulgent work companions, and he did so without the help of our modern 12-step programs. Rather, he continued to peddle his nutrition theory and showed his companions the economic consequences of their decisions. In addition, he offered himself and his own productivity as a powerful social example.

Be Reasonable

Franklin noted in his autobiography that the beatings he received from his brother during his printing apprenticeship gave him a lifetime suspicion of power. In particular, Franklin was suspicious of power as manifested through force. Years after his apprenticeship, Franklin concluded that force and reason are enemies of one another. Further, he suggests that every manager must choose either to be a reasonable manager or a forceful manager.

Here are a few signs that you're working in a force-centered organization instead of a reasonable organization:

- You find yourself making more threats than commitments to your staff.
- You catch yourself saying, "I don't want to hear *your* reasons!"
- You've come to believe that firing employees will solve most of your problems.
- Whoever yells the loudest wins the argument.
- People are afraid of you.
- People would rather do nothing than do the wrong thing.
- Everyone checks with a supervisor before taking any action.
- The only time people call upon reason is to tell you why they *can't* do something.
- You've stopped using monetary incentives to motivate achievement.

Modern managers must make a choice between two attitudes when shaping the culture of their work teams or organizations. On the one hand, you can choose the "my way or the highway" school of management and gain the loyalty and compliance of your employees through fear and intimidation. On the other hand, you can allow reason to rule your business and gain your staff's cooperation through persuasion and self-interest as Franklin did.

"I was now on a fair Footing with them, and soon acquir'd considerable Influence. I propos'd some reasonable Alterations in their [Printing House] Laws, and carried them against all Opposition. From my Example a great Part of them left their muddling Breakfast of Beer & Bread & Cheese, finding they could with me be supply'd from a neighboring House with a large Porringer of hot Water-gruel, sprinkled with Pepper, crumb'd with Bread, & a Bit of Butter in it, for the Price of a Pint of Beer, viz, three half-pence. This was a more comfortable as well as cheaper Breakfast, & kept their Heads clearer. Those who continu'd sotting with Beer all day, were often, by not paying, out of Credit at the Alehouse, and us'd to make Interest with me to get Beer . . . I watch'd the Pay table on Saturday Night, & collected what I stood engag'd for them, having to pay some times near Thirty Shillings a week on their Accounts."

In this example, Franklin neatly demonstrated the power of reason to persuade others to change their behavior. Look again at his two key tactics. First, he suggested a reasonable theory to his colleagues stating that more nutrition can be found in eating bread than drinking beer. Second, he proposed a reasonable alteration in the policy that governed the printing house concerning food and drink. These two simple tactics apparently persuaded the vast majority of his fellow workers away from trying to drink their way to higher productivity. It's worth noting that he coupled these reasonable arguments with the monetary incentive of a cheaper breakfast and lunch. He didn't convert all his fellow workers, but he achieved an admirable degree of success.

How To Make A Bad Decision

In contrast to reason, Franklin identified three other sources of dysfunctional decision-making in his autobiography. He referred to these decision guides using the rather archaic terms "natural inclination, custom and company." I'll discuss these three problem areas using the more modern terms of *passion*, *habit* and *peers*.

In addition to "natural inclination," Franklin often used the term *passion* to describe emotionally-centered decision-making. Not surprisingly, he strongly advised against making decisions based on the passion of the moment. A person led by passion is easier prey for con artists and others who depend on deception in their deal-making. A sure sign that you're operating in the realm of passion is when some-body asks you, Well, do you *feel* like this is a good deal?

This question asks you to disregard reason as a decision-making guide and search your emotions to see if you have a good deal. Any time somebody hands me this phrase when I'm negotiating a deal, a little red flag goes up in my mind. These negotiators want me to base

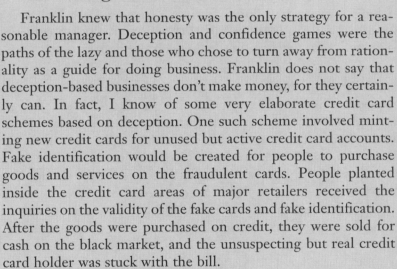

Benjamin Franklin Once Said ...

"Tricks & Treachery are the Practice of Fools, that have not Wit enough to be honest."

Franklin knew that honesty was the only strategy for a rea-sonable manager. Deception and confidence games were the paths of the lazy and those who chose to turn away from ration-ality as a guide for doing business. Franklin does not say that deception-based businesses don't make money, for they certain-ly can. In fact, I know of some very elaborate credit card schemes based on deception. One such scheme involved mint-ing new credit cards for unused but active credit card accounts. Fake identification would be created for people to purchase goods and services on the fraudulent cards. People planted inside the credit card areas of major retailers received the inquiries on the validity of the fake cards and fake identification. After the goods were purchased on credit, they were sold for cash on the black market, and the unsuspecting but real credit card holder was stuck with the bill.

Where are the leaders of this credit card ring? In prison, serving life terms for massive credit card fraud.

In the end, Franklin believed that a business based on tricks and treachery would fall in on itself. Somebody will slip up and give the game away. Somebody will get nervous and squeal to the authorities. The only path to guaranteed business success is honesty. A conscious, rational and imaginative person can real-ly come to no other conclusion.

decisions—*important* decisions—on emotion rather than reason. Although I believe emotion has its place in the world and in decision-making, emotion takes a backseat when confronted with reason.

Habit is a second source of bad decision-making. Habit is a powerful source of behavior patterns, because our habits are often acquired when we're very young and tend to remain unexamined until somebody else points them out to us. It's like being unaware of blinking until somebody points out that you blink about every 10 seconds. Franklin was particularly good at examining his most basic habits in terms of their present effectiveness. What his parents taught him to eat for breakfast or lunch as a child may not be the food that he should have eaten as an adult. In other words, what may have been an effective diet at one point in his life may be ineffective at another. An even better example of Franklin's overcoming the force of habit is his inventing bifocal eyeglasses. Late in his life, Franklin simply tired of switching between two different kinds of spectacles, which was the custom of his day. Consequently, he incorporated both corrections into a single pair of glasses in the first pair of bifocals.

Peers are a final source of bad decision-making. Too many people completely avoid making their own decisions and blindly follow their peers. The rest of us quickly learn that the people we surround ourselves with will be powerful influences on our everyday behavior. Franklin knew that if he socialized with people who were heavy drinkers, he would be more likely to drink. In contrast, he learned that if he made friends with people who liked to read and discuss their ideas, he would probably read more. Therefore, he went to great effort to deliberately surround himself with people who were as self-educating, hard working, frugal and driven by purpose as he was.

When Reason Becomes A God

A word of caution is in order before this chapter ends. Franklin advocated reason to solve a variety of managerial problems, and reason can help you think logically through the problems you face. Reason can rescue you from people who seek to exploit your emotional decision-making. And reason can help you gain the cooperation of your staff through persuasion rather than force. Franklin found reason to be the best tool for navigating the problems faced by managers.

However, when reason becomes a god to be worshipped, you're probably headed for trouble. Although reason might be useful for solving a wide variety of problems at the individual and company levels, dark clouds begin to form on the horizon when reason is made the only criterion for decision-making. Let me offer a rather chilling example. One of the key differences between communist countries like the Soviet Union and capitalist countries like America

The Milk–Cup Terrorist

You can't negotiate with a 2-year-old. This is one of the great universal laws along with "Never corner a wild animal when it's wounded" and "Don't wear white to a spaghetti dinner." My son, Ellis, has taught me a great deal about the limits of reason just by being a normal toddler.

One day Ellis was in a particularly nasty mood. Everything mom and dad tried to do for him only added to his miseries. At one point, he grabbed his milk cup and stomped into the living room for what he hoped would be a personal pity party. We have a rule in our house that milk and juice never leave the kitchen area and you never, ever take these things into the living room. So what do you do when Mr. Don't-Tread-On-Me is holding your couch hostage with his milk cup?

The limits of reason as a problem-solving tool are painfully clear at a time like this. There's no way I could reason with Ellis to hand over the milk cup peacefully. The use of force would be equally disastrous. If I made a move to grab the cup, Ellis would clinch it tighter and the ensuing wrestling match would soak the couch with milk. This is when I reach for the other tool on my managerial tool belt: exchange.

As a human, Ellis has interests just like everybody else. We solved our problem by channeling Ellis' interests to an exchange scenario. Ellis was happy to trade his milk cup for one of his favorite toys when it was offered as an exchange. No milk was spilt, and everybody was left feeling richer than before. When force and reason fail, remember to use exchange.

is that the idea of reason reached godlike status in communist countries.

When reason became a god, bureaucrats in communist countries started to believe that everything could be planned. Bureaucrats were hired to plan what crops were grown in which region of the country and where they would be shipped when harvested. More bureaucrats were hired to plan what kinds of housing would be constructed and who would live in that housing. Everything was planned, and everything was controlled, because the Communists came to believe that the only way to completely master their challenges was to make reason a god.

The Nobel Prize-winning economist Friedrich Hayek called this kind of reason-driven pride the "fatal conceit." It's fatal because every country that has tried to put a completely planned economy into action has effectively destroyed its economy. Witness the history of the former Soviet Union. It's frightening to think that everything seemed reasonable at the time.

This conceit is not limited to nation-states, however. Businesses both large and small can follow the temptation of this fatal conceit when a small group of managers begins thinking that they can plan for every contingency the organization will face and gain the compliance of every worker. When this happens, they have ceased to be managers and have become bureaucrats. Maybe one of the most important questions you could ask yourself is, "Am I running a little Soviet Union or creating a little America?"

What Good Shall I Do This Day?

❏ Choose today to harness reason and self-interest as managerial tools. After all, you live in a capitalist economy.

❏ Use facts and reason to support your ideas. Passion is important, but it doesn't give people the reason they need to give you their support.

❏ Examine your life to find where you act on passion, out of habit or because of peer pressure. See if anything is in need of revision.

❏ Check yourself to determine whether you rely more on force or reason to get things done as a manager.

❏ Remember, reason has its limits. As the size of your business grows so will the complexity of the problems you face.

❏ As your business grows, your best path is to empower your workers to make their own reasonable decisions. You'll never be able to make all their decisions for them.

It was about this time that I conceiv'd the bold and arduous Project of arriving at moral Perfection. I wish'd to live without committing any Fault at any time; I would conquer all that either Natural Inclination, Custom, or Company might lead me into. As I knew, or thought I knew, what was right and wrong, I did not see why I might not always do the one and avoid the other.

—Benjamin Franklin
introducing his plan for
achieving moral perfection

Chapter 7

Becoming A Person Of Value

It's the kind of back-door, tax-free money you've always heard about, and here it is at your back door. You're the manager of a franchised sporting goods resale store in a shopping center in El Paso, Texas, and one of your new employees has just made you a curious offer. You hired Steve because he had owned his own sporting goods store on the East Coast but sold it to move to the cheaper, sunnier Southwest and retire. Soon, however, he got the itch to work again and answered your ad in the local paper. He was the perfect employee for your shop, and after a brief interview, you hired him.

A few weeks after being hired, Steve approaches you with a tempting offer. After he sold his sporting goods business back East, he was left with a significant inventory that the new owner didn't want. It's good stuff, too—shoes, skis, golf clubs and Little League equipment—and it would sell easily at a store like yours. Unfortunately, Steve's plan for selling his inventory doesn't quite fit your franchisor's guidelines.

A Bargain At Just 99 cents!

It's a commonly held belief that pricing an item at 99 cents as opposed to $1 is done for psychological rather than economic reasons. Consumer psychologists contend that there's more than one cent of difference between items priced at $4.99 and at $5. In a similar vein, economists argue that when the price of an item is lowered even one cent, the potential to stimulate sales is enough to recoup the loss on the lower price with higher volume. Savvy managers from the 1700s and 1800s might have another explanation altogether for the existence of such "off dollar" pricing strategies.

Before the invention of the cash register, sales clerks could make a surprising amount of extra money each week by pocketing cash from sales rather than turning the cash over to the owner of the store. Here's how it worked: Let's say that a sales clerk in the late 1800s is helping a wealthy customer pick out a new hat at Marshall Field's in Chicago. The hat sells for a whopping $2 (a lot of money in those days). If the customer purchases the hat, the sales clerk is responsible for handling the cash transaction.

With a sales price of $2, there's a good chance that the customer will simply hand over two $1 bills to the sales clerk and exit the store. At this point, the clerk could easily pocket the money. With "off dollar" pricing strategies placing the hat at $1.99, the clerk is forced to make change from the cash drawer, thereby dramatically increasing the chance of the transaction being accounted for. In those days, it was one more technique managers could use to keep employees honest.

Steve wants to display the inventory on the floor and sell it to regular store customers. However, he doesn't want to enter it into the store database, nor does he want to record the transaction in the accounting system. He wants this to be sold strictly off the record. If anything sells, he'll split the revenue with you 50-50.

The upside of the offer is the easy money. The 50-50 split could mean upwards of $4,000 to $5,000 in your pocket if everything sells. There are downsides to the offer as well, however. Primarily, your franchisor could revoke your franchise agreement if you're caught selling inventory and not recording it in the store records. The franchise agreement includes a percentage of all store revenue for the franchisor. Selling off the record means that those revenues would be unrecorded and, therefore, unpaid to the franchisor. Another downside is the federal income tax evasion issues inherent in this scheme. Using the store to generate business revenue and then not accounting for it is a violation of federal tax laws. Still, the chances of getting caught are slim. So what are you going to tell Steve?

Franklin And The Moral Dilemma

Interestingly enough, Franklin probably faced similar situations in his day. In fact, I suspect he had many situations as franchisee/employee and franchisor/owner-manager. As a journeyman in various printing houses, he probably had many opportunities to take cash for a sale without recording it into his master's records. This problem is one of the oldest in business. Later in his life, Franklin began a series of printing partnerships throughout the American colonies that were very much like modern-day franchise agreements. As such, he would receive a fixed percentage of all accounted revenues. A deceitful partner could easily have skimmed off revenue by not recording every transaction for reporting to Franklin. But Franklin had an excellent method for dealing with moral dilemmas of this kind.

Franklin's Seventh Rule Of Management:
Create your own set of values
to guide your actions.

Simply put, Franklin knew his core personal values, and they guided his decision-making in times of uncertainty. You might think that if you don't know what you value, you really value nothing. This is simply untrue. If you don't know what you value, you will value everything that comes your way. Instead, Franklin had a clearly articulated set of personal values that guided him through difficult decisions. Faced with such a dilemma, he could easily decline Steve's proposition and avoid a personal affront to Steve—an act that might sour their relationship. Rather Franklin was equipped to say no by asking Steve to simply show respect for the personal values that he had chosen to guide his business activity.

What Do You Mean By "Integrity"?

When asked, almost everyone expresses a desire to be a person of integrity. When pressed to define integrity, however, it can be confusing. In a previous career, I was a recruiter for a Fortune 50 oil and gas company. Whenever I heard somebody use the word "integrity" during an interview, I would stop and ask, "So, how do you mean 'integrity'?" The answers would vary: "You know, honest, trustworthy, dependable" and "I mean 'integrity' in the sense of hard working, a promise keeper and always telling the truth" or my personal favorite, "It's, like, being a really, really good person." Although telling the truth was a common theme, it seemed that almost every candidate had different values that defined their integrity, or they just gave the word a glowing halo of goodness without any details whatsoever.

I began thinking about integrity in a new way. Rather than defining integrity as a laundry list of various socially acceptable virtues like dependability or trustworthiness or loyalty, I adopted a more open-ended definition. I now believe that people of integrity act in accordance with the values they profess. Franklin's life offers a remarkable example of this kind of integrity in action. He called his plan for a life of integrity *The Art of Virtue*. At its center was a set of core values that Franklin chose for himself and committed to live by.

Let's go back to the quote on page 98 and review the phrase: "moral perfection." Just let the phrase resonate in your mind for a moment. I've heard my fair share of challenging goals over the years, but moral perfection? Is he serious? During his 20s, Franklin created for himself a list of virtues unique to his time but universal in their challenge. He then began the process of holding himself accountable to these virtues—or behavioral standards—on a daily basis. Each day he pledged to take steps to eradicate one more bad habit from his life. The result—although not moral perfection—was an individual with the habit of self-improvement through goal-setting and feedback on a daily basis.

Values are a necessary part of every human life. Whether or not we acknowledge it, all our decisions and actions are directed by the values we

Benjamin Franklin Once Said ...

"The Master-piece of Man, is to live to the purpose."

Living your life with a clear conceptualization of where you want to end up is what Franklin means by living "...to the purpose." In Chapter 5 we learned that Franklin developed a plan for his entire life when he was still a young man and tried to live up to it. In this chapter, we get the other half of the equation: We need to live purposeful lives with our own set of values.

Before you can clearly see your future, you must clearly see your present. In other words, to get to point B, you must first know the location of point A. We establish point B when we create goals for our lives. We establish point A when we create our own set of values.

Creating your own set of values is a necessary step for getting from point A to point B. Most of us focus solely on point B—our goals or our personal mission statement. We never consider point A. That's unfortunate because point A is where we are today or where we are at the beginning of any new stage in life. Franklin clearly defined both his point A and point B. His point A was his set of personal values that comprised his basic identity. His point B was his plan for his life. Franklin armed himself both with a knowledge of who he was and where he wanted to go. Is it any wonder that he is still studied as a model of effectiveness?

have adopted. Franklin realized early in his life that inner beliefs guide external actions. As such, Franklin chose first to concentrate on the perfectibility of the inner person as a way to perfecting the outer person.

The Art Of Virtue: A Closer Examination

Franklin printed a copy of his plan for moral perfection long before he wrote his autobiography. He called it *The Art of Virtue*, and it was circulated throughout the communities in which Franklin conducted business. In fact, he included it in the autobiography primarily because associates wrote him and encouraged him to find a way to circulate the plan more widely. We owe a debt of thanks to Franklin's friends. Without them, Franklin may not have passed on what is certainly the model for almost all self-improvement programs that followed. Let's take a closer look at how Franklin designed this process.

- **Step 1: Identify and clarify your values.** Before he became a famous actor, Steve Martin was equally famous as a stand-up comedian. He had a routine called "How to Be a Millionaire and Never Pay Taxes." His first step? Get a million dollars! Franklin's legacy leaves us a first step that is equally humorous in both its obviousness and seeming impossibility. To manage in Franklin's footsteps and be a person of value, you must first create your own set of values.

  People who have identified and clearly described their own set of deeply held values are the exception rather than the rule. They are exceptional because the identification and clarification of personal values requires a good deal of reflection and effort. Nevertheless, it is not an impossible task, and several sources yield a ready list of identifiable values that will serve as a starting point. Two immediate sources of values are family cultures and religious experiences. First, try to describe the rules that govern your family life. Is punctuality important? What about healthy lifestyles? Next, focus on your spiritual commitments and religious heritage. What are the central tenets of your faith tradition? Another method I've found that helps people identify specific values is to answer the question, What characteristics do you look for when you consider a spouse, employee or business partner? I find that this question tends to generate some very specific value-laden traits.

Probably the most valuable aid is to see another person's statement of values. The good news is that Franklin left us his own statement of values (see page 106). He lists his 13 core values in order of importance, with temperance listed first,

". . . as it tends to procure that Coolness & Clearness of Head, which is so necessary where constant Vigilance was to be kept up, and Guard maintained, against the unremitting Attraction of ancient Habits, and the Force of perpetual Temptations."

Last on his list is *humility*, which he added at the insistence of a Quaker friend who informed him that he was generally thought to be a proud person. Having no real ownership of the value but a genuine disgust of the effect pride was having on his public reputation,

The End Of The World As We Know It

Whenever I am asked to help people identify and clarify their values, I've found forced-choice scenarios to be very useful. You know forced choice as the popular lifeboat dilemma that asks you which six or seven people out of a group of 15 would you put into a lifeboat. These lifeboat scenarios are very good at helping people decide whether a child who will grow up to find a cure for diabetes is more important to them than the president of an advertising agency who, if rescued, will die two years later of diabetes.

Here's an easy and more modern dilemma that might help: Suppose that a large asteroid is on a collision course with Earth, and complete destruction is assured in a matter of weeks. You have been given the opportunity to save 100 people from this destruction. What kind of people will you select? If you choose primarily family members, there's a good chance that family is one of your central values. If you choose artists and musicians, maybe you value a world of beauty. If you choose scientists, it could be that progress and discovery are important to you. The more specific you can be about the 100 people you will save, the more effective you will be at isolating your own individual values.

Benjamin Franklin's Creed And List Of Virtues

That there is One God, who made all things. That He governs the world by His Providence. That He ought to be worshipped with adoration, prayer, and thanksgiving. But that the most acceptable service of God is doing good to men. That the soul is immortal. And that God will certainly reward virtue and punish vice, either here or hereafter.

Temperance
Eat not to Dullness. Drink not to Elevation.

Silence
Speak not but what may benefit others or yourself.
Avoid trifling Conversation.

Order
Let all your Things have their Places. Let each Part of your Business have its Time.

Resolution
Resolve to perform what you ought. Perform without fail what you resolve.

Frugality
Make no Expense but to do good to others or yourself:
i.e., Waste nothing.

Industry
Lose no Time. Be always employ'd in something useful.
Cut off all unnecessary Actions.

Sincerity
Think innocently and justly; and, if you speak,
speak accordingly.

Justice
Wrong none, by doing Injuries or omitting the Benefits that are your Duty.

Moderation
Avoid Extremes. Forbear resenting Injuries so much as you think they deserve.

Cleanliness
Tolerate no Uncleanness in Body, Clothes or Habitation.

Tranquillity
Be not disturbed at Trifles, or at Accidents common
or unavoidable.

Chastity
Rarely use Venery but for Health or Offspring;
Never to Dullness, Weakness, or the Injury of your own
or another's Peace or Reputation.

Humility
Imitate Jesus and Socrates.

Franklin sought to eliminate this character flaw immediately. In the end, Franklin admitted that he could not "... boast much Success in acquiring the Reality of this Virtue; but I had a good deal with regard to the Appearance of it."

- **Step 2: Turn your values into behavioral goals.** Franklin did more than just create a list of values. He took his values and turned them into daily, measurable goals. For example, he made the virtue of temperance measurable by the definition "Eat not to Dullness. Drink not to Elevation." If Franklin were to consume too much alcohol, his drunkenness would be a clear indicator of his failure to adhere to this virtue.

Franklin was not always so specific with his behavioral goals. In fact, his behavioral goal for the virtue of humility was the rather intimidating (and rather general): "Imitate Jesus and Socrates." As noted above, he privately believed he harbored a great deal of pride in spite of his efforts to imitate two of the most important and genuinely humble figures in Western civilization. Given all the information in Chapter 4, it's hard to believe that Franklin failed to act in genuinely humble ways with other people. However, this is not the standard by which he measured himself. Had he measured himself by a different standard, such as avoiding language that suggests a fixed opinion on a matter like the words "certainly" and "undoubtedly," then he may have perceived himself to be more successful. Thus, you should try to avoid general, nonmeasurable results when developing a personal value statement and seek instead to have specific measurable results.

- **Step 3: Set up a monitoring and feedback system.** To keep himself accountable for his values and goals, Franklin created a feedback sheet with the days of the week across the top and his values in rows down the side.

> "I determined to give a Week's strict Attention to each of the Virtues successively. Thus in the first Week my great Guard was to avoid every the least Offense against Temperance, leaving the other Virtues to their ordinary Chance, only marking every Evening the Faults of the Day. Thus if in the first Week I could keep my first Line marked T (for Temperance) clear of Spots, I suppos'd the Habit of that Virtue so much strengthen'd and its opposite weaken'd, that I might venture extending my Attention to include the next, and for the following Week keep both Lines clear of Spots. Proceeding thus to the last, I could go thro' a Course complete in Thirteen Weeks, and four Courses in a Year."

Franklin tackled this project with his typical deliberateness and moderation. Notice that he didn't try to master all 13 values at once. Rather, he started with the first one the first week. Each evening he reflected on his day to determine which values he failed to live up to, with special attention on the first value, temperance. If he could keep the feedback sheet free of marks for a week, then he assumed mastery of temperance and proceeded to add the next value on the list. He continued this process for 13 weeks to cover all values, and he could do the course four times per year.

- **Step 4: Be prepared for failure.** What!? Franklin's example shows us that the only failure in self-management is the failure to attempt to manage yourself. He would never achieve the moral perfection that he sought through such a plan. Yet he would gain something from the exercise. He wrote, ". . . tho' I never arrived at the Perfection I had been so ambitious of obtaining, but fell far short of it, yet I was by the Endeavor a better and happier Man than I otherwise would have been, if I had not attempted it."

Grand visions, like moral perfection, are inspiring but notoriously difficult to implement. People who strive for grand visions such as zero defects, 100 percent market share, world peace or moral perfection often find that their goals are unattainable. Nonetheless, the existence of the grand vision and the focused effort spent in trying to attain the goal will often result in a vastly improved product.

- **Step 5: Be prepared for criticism.** In the end, Franklin concluded that it was undesirable to have a perfect character—or at least the perception of a perfect character. He states that, ". . . a perfect character might be attended to with the inconvenience of being envied and hated; and that a benevolent man should allow a few faults in himself, to keep his friends in countenance." Franklin was wise enough to realize the power of other people's envy to create problems in your life. It's not just a person of perfect character who will be a target of envy. Rather, it's anybody who even *attempts* the process of character perfection who will be ridiculed.

The Metric-Driven Company

The Dell Computer Co. is one of the great entrepreneurial success stories of the Digital Age. One key to its success lies in its willingness to clarify key corporate values, create ways to measure them and provide the feedback to the members of the organization. Dell refers to this as being a "metric-driven company." Others, like Intel, refer to it as being a "data-driven company."

How does it work? Michael Dell and his management team identify the firm's corporate values and strategic initiatives for the year. For example, central to Dell's mission is to meet customer expectations. Isn't this everyone's mission? Well, no, and Dell actually measures its success in meeting customer expectations with objective criteria in a variety of areas such as quality, service, pricing and technological leadership. The feedback from customers is then communicated both to individual Dell employees and in consolidated forms to the firm's management. Any necessary adjustments are made, vision and initiatives are reconsidered, and the process begins again. As a result, Dell does better than almost any other computer manufacturer in providing customers with just the experience they expected . . . and the customers keep coming back.

A perfect example of such envy came a century later when the novelist D.H. Lawrence wrote an angry attack both of Franklin as a human being and the process described in *The Art of Virtue*. Lawrence was a modern novelist who became disenchanted with humankind and society in general following World War I. Lawrence wrote about Franklin in his book *Studies in Classic American Literature*, which began with the lines, "The Perfectibility of Man! Ah, heaven, what a dreary theme!" He went on to criticize Franklin's beliefs in self-education, self-management and reason. The centerpiece of Lawrence's work was a mockery of Franklin's creed and statement of personal values. Lawrence's creed and values can be found on page 112, demonstrating the nature of the attack.

Lawrence's critique of Franklin will have some appeal to many modern readers. Further, some of Lawrence's creativity might be an asset in turbulent business environments that demand innovation

BHAG Yourself

im Collins and Jerry Porras addressed the subject of grand visions such as moral perfection in their bestselling book, *Built to Last: Successful Habits of Visionary Companies*. In that book, they created one of the latest and most linguistically unpalatable business buzzwords, BHAG (pronounced BEE-hag). BHAG stands for big, hairy, audacious goals; and Porras and Collins found most companies that survive in the long run have them at the center of their organizational mission.

BHAG are never really attained, much like Benjamin Franklin's ideal of moral perfection. Yet, BHAG differentiate winners from losers by providing successful companies a target to continually chase. None of the companies labeled as winners by Collins and Porras ever admitted to completely achieving their BHAG, and a few of the companies even changed their BHAG. In contrast, firms studied by Collins and Porras that set reasonable goals and achieved them year after year tended to flounder more than firms with BHAG. If continued forward momentum is a foundation of competitiveness, then BHAG seem to provide fuel for the competitive engine.

and contrarian attitudes as a means of survival. Lawrence's attack is not included here as a condemnation of what he has done. Rather, it's included to demonstrate the kind of criticism and mockery you can expect if you start down this road.

Honesty Is Still The Best Policy

Although it's not explicitly stated as a core value in his *Art of Virtue* writings, Franklin had a deep commitment to honesty in business dealings. In fact, it could very well be the one core value he left out of his *Art of Virtue* program. His commitment to honesty permeates much of the autobiography and many other of his public and personal writings. In the autobiography, he tells the story of the time he and a group of childhood friends stole some stones from a local construction site to build a platform for themselves in a beloved, but rather marshy, play place. Franklin recounts how the deed was discovered and the lessons he learned.

> "The next Morning the Workmen were surpris'd at Missing the Stones; which were found in our Wharf; Inquiry was made after the Removers; we were discovered & complain'd of; several of us were corrected by our Fathers; and tho' I pleaded the Usefulness of the Work, mine convinc'd me that nothing was useful which was not honest."

In Chapter 5, Franklin cited industry, or hard work, and frugality as the primary *individual* virtues every citizen needs. Later in the autobiography, Franklin professed honesty as his primary *social* virtue. Whereas effective people tend to be distinguished by their hard work and frugality, effective societies tend to be distinguished by their social commitment to honesty. In recounting the story of the publication and influence of his very successful *Poor Richard's Almanac*, Franklin noted:

> "In 1732 I first published my Almanack under the name of Richard Saunders; it was continu'd by me about 25 Years, commonly call'd Poor Richard's Almanack. I endeavor'd to make it both entertaining and useful, and it accordingly came to be in such Demand that I reap'd considerable Profit from it, vending annually near ten Thousand. And observing that it was generally read, scarce any Neighborhood in the Province being with-

D.H. Lawrence's Creed And List Of Virtues

That I am I. That my soul is a dark forest. That my known self will never be more than a little clearing in the forest. That gods, strange gods, come forth from the forest into the clearing of my known self, and then go back. That I must have the courage to let them come and go. That I will never let mankind put anything over me, but that I will try always to recognize and submit to the gods in me and the gods in other men and women.

Temperance
Eat and carouse with Bacchus, or munch dry bread with Jesus, but don't sit down without one of the gods.

Silence
Be still when you have nothing to say; when genuine passion moves you, say what you've got to say, and say it hot.

Order
Know that you are responsible for the gods inside you and to the men in whom the gods are manifest. Recognize your superiors and your inferiors, according to the gods. This is the root of all order.

Resolution
Resolve to abide by your own deepest promptings, and to sacrifice the smaller thing to the greater. Kill when you must, and be killed the same: the must coming from the gods inside you, or from the men in whom you recognize the Holy Ghost.

Frugality
Demand nothing; accept what you see fit. Don't waste your pride or squander your emotion.

Industry
Lose no time with ideals; serve the Holy Ghost; never serve mankind.

Sincerity
To be sincere is to remember that I am I, and that the other man is not me.

Justice
The only justice is to follow the sincere intuition of the soul,
angry or gentle. Anger is just, and pity is just,
but judgment is never just.

Moderation
Beware of absolutes. There are many gods.

Cleanliness
Don't be too clean. It impoverishes the blood.

Tranquillity
The soul has many motions, many gods come and go. Try to
find your deepest issue, in every confusion, and abide by that.
Obey the man in whom you recognize the Holy Ghost;
command when your honour comes to command.

Chastity
Never "use" venery at all. Follow your passional impulse,
if it be answered in the other being; but never have any motive
in mind, neither offspring nor health nor even pleasure, nor
even service. Only know that "venery" is of the great gods. An
offering-up of yourself to the very great gods, the dark ones,
and nothing else.

Humility
See all men and women according to the Holy Ghost that is
within them. Never yield before the barren.

out it, I consider'd it as a proper Vehicle for conveying Instruction among the common People, who bought scarce any other Books. I therefore filled all the little Spaces that occurr'd between the Remarkable Days in the Calendar, with Proverbial Sentences, chiefly such as inculcated Industry and Frugality, as the Means of procuring Wealth and thereby securing Virtue, it being more difficult for a Man in Want to act always honestly, as (to use here one of those Proverbs) 'it is hard for an empty Sack to stand upright.'"

Franklin suggests that the key moral problem in society is getting everybody to "act always honestly." This is true for businesses as well as societies. Imagine a business staffed with people who never keep their promises and create elaborate frauds to steal money from other departments. Such a business will never create any wealth but rather will shift existing wealth from department to department. Further, the deceit underlying such a redistribution process will foster incredible amounts of hate and suspicion among workgroups.

Franklin goes on to suggest that if people don't accept the necessity of honesty from a moral standpoint, they may be persuaded through their pocketbooks to live more honest lives. When he states that it's hard for an empty sack to stand upright, he means that a person without money is more likely to engage in dishonest acts than a person with money. Desperate people resort to desperate measures, so Franklin suggested first helping people obtain wealth by teaching them that hard work and frugality lead to wealth. Therefore, properly used monetary incentives may be an excellent means of promoting honesty and domestic peace in a society or business.

The End Of The Matter

So whatever happened to D.H. Lawrence, anyway? After all, he condemned Franklin so harshly that we at least need to see if his set of values led to better results than the ones he hated so much. Interestingly, Lawrence was British by birth but lived in America—land of Franklin—for much of his adult life. Let's take a quick look at the final resting places of both Franklin and Lawrence.

The final resting place of D.H. Lawrence is purportedly in the western United States just outside Taos, New Mexico, where he owned some ranch land and lived. In his latter years, Lawrence became increasingly ill with tuberculosis and moved back to Europe to seek medical help. Lawrence died while in Europe, and his body was eventually cremated. His ashes were to be used to build a monument on a hillside overlooking northern New Mexico. Unfortunately, most people suspect that his ashes were dumped by the person designated to carry them back to the United States so as to avoid the expense and trouble of transporting them across the Atlantic.

Nonetheless, the carrier is believed to have procured some new ashes upon his arrival in New York, and these were used to construct a monument at Lawrence's ranch in northern New Mexico. The monument can be visited if you are willing to travel a bit off the road. In the end, D.H. Lawrence died an early death as a tormented and rather lonely man. The only monument to his life (aside from his literary

Benjamin Franklin Once Said...

"How few there are who have courage enough to own their Faults, or resolution enough to mend them."

In the end, being a person of value is about being humble enough to identify and correct your faults. A personal value statement will provide you with a great deal of decision-making power and will lead you to a clear sense of personal mission. However, it will also illuminate your shortcomings.

Franklin began this process with the intention of achieving moral perfection by both establishing positive habits and eliminating negative ones. An easy temptation is to accept the idea of developing positive habits, like exercise or reading or eating with moderation, while avoiding the elimination of negative habits. Things that are hard to do or unsavory are usually great sources of competitive advantage, however. For example, maintaining a spotlessly clean environment is extremely hard work, yet the Walt Disney Co. manages to turn this tough task into a key source of competitive advantage.

Franklin may have risen to the heights that he did because he fought the battle for virtue on both the positive and negative end. While many were content with developing positive habits, Franklin went further to eliminate negative ones. So if everybody around you is doing the positive thing, and nobody is distinctive as a result of this, your future is most likely in facing down your faults and improving on them. For example, if everyone in your industry has great products but can't keep their delivery promises, the first company that manages to do both consistently will triumph.

contributions) is one that is built at his own ranch. There was no out-pouring of public sentiment when he died, and only a small group mourned his passing.

Like Lawrence, Franklin left very specific instructions in his will for his burial. Franklin died peacefully in his sleep in the home of his daughter Sarah after a long and distinguished life. He specifically instructed that he be buried with as little expense as possible. He also requested that he be laid to rest next to his wife beneath a simple marble stone with the inscription: "Benjamin and Deborah Franklin: 1790." Unlike Lawrence's death, Franklin's passing was headline news, and he was mourned the world over.

In contrast to Lawrence, who built a private monument to himself, the citizens of America have erected multiple public monuments to Franklin in Philadelphia, Boston and elsewhere. He is one of the few non-presidents to appear on American currency. Franklin's primary goal was to serve his fellow citizen and, in the end, the citizens chose to memorialize his image. In the end, Franklin's values seemed to have led to the more significant and honorable end.

What Good Shall I Do This Day?

❑ Choose your own personal values to guide your life and decisions. They will be your compass in times of uncertainty.

❑ Justify your ethical decisions by pointing to your personal values rather than risk offending others by seizing the moral high ground.

❑ Challenge all your co-workers to develop their own value statements. Be prepared for some people to go elsewhere if they do this clarifying exercise.

❑ Aim for perfection. Even though you'll fail, the improvement from the effort will be better than if you never aimed for perfection.

❑ Make each value a measurable behavioral goal. Track your progress to mark how this value starts to develop in your life.

❑ Don't be alarmed when other people criticize you. Encourage them to clarify their own positions into personal value statements.

❑ Make a radical commitment to being honest in all business transactions and situations.

We had for our Chaplain a zealous Presbyterian Minister, Mr. Beatty, who complain'd to me that the Men did not generally attend his Prayers & Exhortations. When they enlisted, they were promis'd, besides Pay & Provisions, a Gill of Rum a Day, which was punctually serv'd out to them half in the Morning and the other half in the Evening, and I observ'd they were as punctual in attending to receive it. Upon which I said to Mr. Beatty, 'It is perhaps below the Dignity of your Profession to act as Steward of the Rum. But if you were to deal it out and only just after Prayers, you would have them all about you.' He lik'd the Thought, undertook the Office, and with the help of a few hands to measure out the Liquor executed it to Satisfaction; and never were Prayers more generally & more punctually attended. So that I thought this Method preferable to the Punishments inflicted by some military Laws for Non-Attendance on Divine Service.

—Benjamin Franklin
noting the power of incentive and
the limitations of punishments

Chapter 8

Incentive
Is Everything

et's suppose you've just taken a job as a drilling manager for an international oil and gas firm. Your first assignment is jump-starting an abandoned drilling rig deep in the wilds of Siberia. The available labor pool consists of local backwoodsmen who have a rudimentary knowledge of the drilling technology because they operated the crude rigs of the fallen communist regime. Your workers are familiar with the process, which is good, even though the Russian technology is 40 years behind the rest of the world.

Unfortunately, however, they also have a love of vodka. In fact, their idea of a good day at work includes buying all the vodka they can afford and drinking until incapacitated. In contrast, your idea of a good day at work is making continued downward progress on your oil well. It's clear that the goals of the manager and the workers diverge. One more limitation: You're stuck with these guys because your government contract requires you to employ Russian workers. What can you do as a manager to further the goals of your company?

Rewarding The Franklin Way

Benjamin Franklin believed strongly in the power of rewards for altering behavior. In the opening quote above, the military chaplain, Mr. Beatty, wanted the militia members to attend prayers because he thought it was right, and it was his job to conduct the prayers. According to the militia rules, all members were supposed to attend. When they didn't attend, his job as chaplain became frustrating.

Ever the practical problem solver, Franklin simply looked for the activity which most interested the men and which they were most punctual in attending. Thus, he discovered that they rarely missed their twice daily serving of rum. All that remained was to tie the reward to the desired behavior. Franklin suggested that the chaplain be put in charge of giving out the rum and distribute it only at the completion of the evening teaching and prayer service. It's surprising that the chaplain had the humility of office to try this solution. It's no surprise, however, for Franklin to note that prayers were never better attended.

Franklin's Eighth Rule Of Management:
Incentive is everything.

Franklin's solution for the managerial challenge in the Siberian oil patch might be somewhat similar to his solution with the Colonial militia. The key to solving the problem is in tying rewards to desired behaviors. The manager wants continued downward progress on the oil well; the workers want vodka and time off to drink. A classic Franklin solution might be to reward a certain number of feet drilled each day with a certain amount of vodka for the workers.

Although this might be a classic Franklin solution, it's probably not the best solution. Given the inherent dangers of working on an oil rig, it's probably good policy to separate the work from alcohol consumption, especially company-sponsored alcohol consumption. Therefore, it might be more prudent to pay the workers in cash whenever a certain drilling goal is met. The sooner the workers meet the goal each day, the sooner they can leave the rig. Then, if they choose to spend their cash on vodka, it is their own liability.

Probably the worst managerial mistake you could make in this situation would be to try to manage the vodka problem in hopes it would disappear, resulting in productivity gains. Chances are that the absence of vodka would not guarantee continued downward progress on the well. It might guarantee a sober work force, and this is indeed a desirable outcome. However, the workers will be more inclined to drill if they are rewarded for drilling. This is known as self-interest, and it's the subject of the next section.

The Most Powerful Motivator

In 1734, Franklin wrote this advice in *Poor Richard's Almanac*: "Would you persuade, speak of interest not of reason." As a child of the Enlightenment, Franklin believed strongly in the power of reason (Chapter 6 was devoted to discussing his views on reason), but he also believed, however, in one force more powerful than reason. That force was self-interest.

A contemporary of Franklin's, Adam Smith, wrote extensively about the power of self-interest and the wisdom of developing institutions that harness its power for the common good. Smith wrote in *The Wealth of Nations* that it wasn't from the benevolence of the butcher, brewer or baker that we could expect our dinner tonight. Rather, they did their part to prepare our dinner as a result of their own self-interest. A butcher would slaughter cattle all day—a very distasteful job— only if he expected that customers would pay him for his services.

Neither Smith nor Franklin contended that we are motivated solely by our self-interest. It's clear from the autobiography that Franklin finds both himself and others motivated by factors like love, altruism and reason. However, Smith and Franklin would agree that self-interest motivates more powerfully and more consistently in the general population than just about any other factor. Therefore, it's wishful thinking to hope that humankind is motivated solely by the noblest desires. Rather, the manager's task is to use the most consistently powerful motivator—self-interest—to the best possible advantage.

Let's contrast the idea that workers are motivated by self-interest with four other common models of worker motivation. Although the self-interest explanation is not perfect, I promote it because the other four perspectives suffer from more serious flaws.

- **The good soldier model:** This view of employee management assumes that every employee has a heightened sense of duty and loyalty and will act in the interest of the company because it is every employee's basic duty to do so. Although downsizing has wreaked havoc on employee loyalty in the past decade, there's a glimmer of loyalty in most employees. Ultimately, however, it's naive to assume that employees will promote the interests of the company in the absence of monetary rewards. It may happen; just don't bet on it.

- **The victim of the environment model:** This behavioral school of thought assumes that every action by an employee is a reaction to a stimulus in the employee's environment. The logical conclusion is that employees are perfectible if their environment is engineered properly and they are appropriately socialized. Although this viewpoint has some validity, it ultimately strips the power of choice from employees. Rewards and punishments are indeed powerful in altering human behavior, but people are far more creative and clever than this model credits them as being.

- **The happy is productive model:** This viewpoint promotes the idea that happy employees are productive. In such a model, the manager creates an environment that maximizes employee happiness, then sits back and watches productivity skyrocket. If you followed this logic in the opening problem, a manager would be expected to provide plenty of satisfying vodka before making any productivity demands. This approach will result in the management of employee emotion rather than the management of employee productivity. Management of employee satisfaction will be discussed later in this chapter. The shortcomings of this viewpoint were thoroughly discussed in Chapter 5.

- **The therapeutic model:** The therapeutic approach to management views the lack of productivity and other workplace ills as diseases to be diagnosed and cured, primarily through counseling and prescription drugs. Totally psychological in nature, the therapeutic model seeks to change the individual rather than the environment. Managers working from this viewpoint are quick to enroll employees in employee assistance programs, hoping for the breakthrough intervention that restores their on-the-job productivity. Common diagnoses in this managerial model are depression, attention deficit disorder and anxiety attacks.

The four management models above all have some truth associated with them. Employees often go above and beyond the call of duty on the job without extra pay, demonstrating the merit of the good soldier model. Manic-depressive employees find help in employee assistance programs and return to the workplace to make sound contributions to the bottom line. Franklin, however, viewed the individual employee as a powerful resource to be leveraged

Benjamin Franklin Once Said...

"Hope of gain lessens pain."

Effort. That's the magic word. Every manager must find ways to motivate employees to exert effort. Effort is required when we face a distasteful task. Thus, it is important to match the personalities and interests of employees to the demands of jobs. For example, extroverts tend to enjoy sales more than shy, introverted people, so managers should avoid placing extremely bashful and nonsocial people in jobs requiring a great deal of human interaction.

Not all distasteful tasks can be avoided, however. Franklin advises leveraging the promise of monetary gain to lessen the prospect of personal discomfort associated with any particular job. Even bashful people are more likely to engage in conversation when they know that they can improve their financial standing as a result of a little initiative and conversation.

and the employee's self-interest as the most powerful motivator. Through the skillful use of incentive management, Franklin established this viable approach for managers.

How To Link Pay To Performance

One of Franklin's most important legacies—the one that earns him the title Founding Father of American Business—is the powerful link that he established between effort and reward in the American cultural experience. His story of "rags to riches" and the "self-made man" is chronicled in his autobiography for all American generations that followed. He started with little and gained much through hard work and persistence. Franklin demonstrated that the right kind of effort is ultimately rewarded in the American experience.

An incentive system establishing a link between pay and performance is one of a manager's most important tasks. Truly effective pay systems remind all participants on a daily basis that hard work is rewarded. Managers must pay close attention to three linkages to maximize the impact of any company's compensation system.

● **The link between effort and performance:** This link is the connection between harder work and higher performance. It has nothing to do with reward outcomes; that is the next step in the process. The first order of business in building a solid system of high performance is helping all members of the organization learn to improve their performance by exerting effort.

Franklin recorded many linkages between personal effort and higher performance in his autobiography. These include most of the previously discussed stories about self-education and self-management. In the end, Franklin firmly believed that if he worked harder (effort) he would do better (performance). If your employees do not share this fundamental belief, almost any effort to improve performance in your business will fail.

● **The link between performance and reward:** After building a foundation between effort and performance, a manager's next task is to ensure that proper performance is rewarded. Franklin noted many occasions in his life when higher performance was rewarded. For example, his mastery of the Socratic method of persuasion resulted in his being able to influence more people to accept his point of view. Also, his clever public relations campaign for more paper currency resulted in his being rewarded with the contract to print the money in his print shop.

Commission-based compensation systems are excellent examples of linking performance to reward. A salesperson is rewarded only when a sale is made. Although commission-based compensation systems can be harsh taskmasters, they are proven systems for increasing the level of sales in any organization. The same can be said for stock-based compensation systems for top

Why Not Just Link Effort And Reward?

Isn't it too nit-picky to distinguish between the link of effort and performance and that of performance and reward? Not at all! Without this distinction, a manager is forced to link effort and reward. Simply put, this is a recipe for disaster in a capitalist economy. It's a disaster because you're creating a system that rewards effort rather than performance.

As a college professor, I make a conscientious effort every semester to avoid rewarding students merely for exerting effort. Time after time, students come to my office and complain about a low grade on an assignment. The complaint is always the same: "But I worked for *hours* on that assignment!" I try to be sympathetic and encouraging, but I firmly point out that the assignment was not done correctly. My most important job at this point is to help students effectively rechannel their effort so that it results in higher performance or a correctly solved problem.

Effort is a necessary component in any high-performance work system, and employees ultimately control how much effort they wish to exert at work. However, effort for the sake of effort alone will probably never lead to higher performance. Any employee can demonstrate effort by working longer hours or increasing work activity to a frantic pace. Unfocused effort is dangerous, however. A manager must create a system that transforms effort into organizationally beneficial performance and then reward the performance that results.

managers. The only route to higher pay (or sometimes any pay at all) is to increase the performance—or the stock price—of the business.

● **The link between reward and employee values:** One final linkage is necessary when creating high-performance work systems: the link between what an employee values and what rewards a business offers. Most employees value money because money provides them with a wide variety of exchange options. However, some rewards like status or recognition are not monetary.

Nonvalued rewards can be dysfunctional for the business. When Mary Kay Ash worked for Stanley Home Products, she won their national sales contest one year. And what was her reward for that increase in performance? Some fishing gear! Probably one of the least valued rewards she could have received as a middle-aged woman in the 1960s. Her hard work in reaching new customers and improving relationships with existing ones resulted in greater sales and should have resulted in greater rewards. Unfortunately Stanley dropped the ball in the end by rewarding her with something she cared little for. Ash notes in her autobiography that this was a turning point in her life and a loss for Stanley Home Products, as she left to establish her own legendary business.

In this chapter's opening quotation, Franklin leverages something of value (rum) to reward desired performance (attendance at prayer service). That anecdote demonstrates all the linkages necessary for better performance. Individual effort on the part of the militia volunteers to attend prayer service is clearly observable as higher performance, and the improved performance is promptly rewarded at the conclusion of the prayer service by something the militiamen value.

Franklin found this reward system preferable to the more common military solution of punishments for non-attendance at religious services. It's not surprising that a bureaucracy like the military would reach for a force-based solution instead of an interest-based solution. Is reward a more powerful and effective motivator than punishment? Franklin offers little more than his informed opinion after observing a pattern of behaviors, but modern behavioral science has thoroughly investigated the question, and the answer is most intriguing.

Benjamin Franklin Once Said ...

"Without justice, courage is weak."

"Pardoning the Bad, is injuring the Good."

Justice is a managerial concept that we don't hear much about anymore. That's unfortunate, too, since even Superman fought for truth, justice and the American way. In the broadest sense, *justice* is a social contract promising that all members of an organization should be the beneficiary of what is rightfully theirs. For example, justice demands that salespeople receive credit and compensation for the sales that they complete in a certain time period. To compensate one salesperson with commission pay for the work done by another salesperson is injustice in its most basic form.

The same goes for rewarding people with a bonus when they do no work or less work than required. For example, let's say that a manager has a productivity push where the top performer gets an extra day of paid vacation. However, the manager was so pleased with the results that he gave *all* employees who took part an extra day off. While this will win the manager the loyalty of the lower performers, it will alienate him from the top performer who must now share the reward with everyone.

Whether we are aware of it or not, justice is the foundation of risk-taking in any organizational effort. If employees do not see the link between risk and reward in your firm, you will quickly have a company full of risk-avoiders. Risk avoidance can come as a result of watching a co-worker come up with a new revenue-generating or cost-saving idea and then somebody else getting the credit and monetary bonus for the idea. On the other hand, when workers see that they can individually capture the rewards of effort, imagination and risk-taking, then you're likely to see it flower. Management exists, in part, to administer organizational justice. Without it, you may find that your organization is full of cowards.

What's For Dinner, Dr. Skinner?

One of the most prominent and controversial behavioral science researchers of the 20th century was Dr. B.F. Skinner. (Note: B.F. stands for Burrhus Frederic, not Benjamin Franklin.) As a psychologist, B.F. Skinner is considered to be second in influence only to Sigmund Freud. His primary contribution is having popularized the school of psychological thought known as behaviorism.

Typical reactions to the mention of Skinner's name include remarks such as "Skinner? Isn't he the fellow who thinks that people are robots?" and, "Skinner believed people are just puppet-like rats in mazes controlled by some mastermind who pulls the strings." True, in retrospect, Skinner had a rather limited conceptualization of human beings, which casual readers may interpret as robotic. True, Dr. Skinner conducted much of his research with animals such as rodents and birds, and he used mazes. In his defense, however, he could get those rats and pigeons to do some amazing tricks!

Skinner developed the concept of operant conditioning, which suggests that all behavior is a response to the stimuli present in the subject's environment. Typical Skinnerian experiments include teaching a pigeon to ring a bell with its beak when a particular light blinks and teaching a rat to navigate increasingly difficult mazes. Skinner succeeded in these studies primarily by rewarding the animal subjects with food pellets when they demonstrated the desired behaviors.

One benefit of Skinner's work to the practicing manager is that he came to some rather precise and well-documented conclusions about the power of both rewards and punishment in changing behavior. Skinner believed that most behaviors fell into two categories: desirable and undesirable. How does a manager elicit desirable behaviors like productivity and friendly service and extinguish undesirable behaviors like laziness and rudeness? Skinner's answer after decades of systematic observation confirms Franklin's more casual observations about the correlation between men attending prayer services and the distribution of rum.

Skinner found that rewards tend to be far more powerful than punishments in eliciting desired behaviors. Did Skinner find that punish-

Other People's Money

Franklin learned early in life that incentive is everything in managing money. Specifically, he learned that you are never as careful when managing other people's money as you are when managing your own. During some of his early travels, he received a sizable sum of money from an acquaintance of one of his brothers. As receiver, Franklin was charged with safeguarding the money until it was called for by his brother's friend. Following the receipt of the money, Franklin unwisely chose to use some of the funds to finish financing his trip back to Philadelphia.

Worse yet, Franklin allowed a friend of his to use some of the money. This particular friend had a drinking problem and returned often for more money, always promising to pay the money back soon. Ultimately, the relationship between the two friends went sour. Franklin's friend departed for Barbados with a promise to repay after he received money from his new employment, but Franklin never heard from him again. Franklin later classified this mismanagement of funds as the first great mistake of his life. Fortunately for Franklin, his brother's friend did not call for the money for several years, giving Franklin ample time to replenish the funds.

ment alters behavior? Absolutely. In fact, he found that you could extinguish undesirable behaviors in subjects by punishing them. But Skinner found that rewards are twice as effective as punishments in eliciting desired behaviors. He demonstrated that when a subject was rewarded for exhibiting a desired behavior instead of punished for exhibiting an undesirable behavior, the subject learned the desired behavior twice as fast, and the behavior tended to persist twice as long. In other words, although punishment can change behavior, rewards tend to work more quickly and be more effective in the long run. Although Skinner could not gather emotional data on his rodent subjects, he would probably have also found that they enjoyed the rewards a great deal more than the punishments and had more positive feelings about receiving rewards.

Incentive Is Everything
At Prime Time Shuttle

The power of rewards to motivate exceptional performance is one of the foundations of capitalism, and capitalism is nowhere better exemplified than at Prime Time Shuttle in Los Angeles. Prime Time Shuttle provides door-to-door ground transportation to and from airports. A legitimate starving actor named John Kindt started Prime Time in Los Angeles in the early 1980s. During the past 15 years, Prime Time Shuttle has grown to be one of the dominant airport shuttle companies in the greater Los Angeles area.

Prime Time Shuttle sought only to provide airline travelers an alternative to taking their personal cars to the airport, and they have discovered that travelers do indeed demand this service. Further, they have been able to consistently deliver customers on time for well under the cost of a taxi. One key to Prime Time's effectiveness is its incentive system.

Prime Time Shuttle doesn't employ any hourly or salaried van drivers. The people who drive vans for Prime Time are known as owner-operators. Here's how it works: People who want to drive for Prime Time Shuttle actually purchase their vans, equipment and services from Prime Time. They pay a flat rate plus a percentage of their revenues for using the Prime Time brand name.

The system is very similar to a franchise except it operates at the level of the individual employee. As in a franchise system, owner-operators keep all the revenue that exceeds the fixed and variable charges owed to Prime Time Shuttle. Thus, a great incentive exists for the owner-operator to generate additional revenue by working longer hours, earning higher tips for better service and minimizing inefficient downtime and side trips.

Similarly, safety incentives benefit owner-operators, passengers and society, because owner-operators are personally responsible for damages resulting from recklessness. Prime Time's system is laudable for providing incentives for growth, efficiency and safety while avoiding the disadvantages associated with traditional employment relationships and wage-based payment plans.

Benjamin Franklin Once Said ...

"Mine is better than Ours."

Private property is one of the foundations of a free market economy and of effective management. Private property is effective in the marketplace because it allows people to receive all the benefits of owning a particular piece of land or structure or idea. Ownership provides the incentive people need to be good stewards of what is under their control.

The concept of private property can also be effective in the workplace through personal ownership of items necessary to your business. For example, it's a longstanding practice for construction workers to provide their own tools at the work site. This policy evolved from earlier experiments in which managers provided workers with building tools and discovered that the rather expensive tools were used carelessly and were poorly maintained. The solution was to require workers to bring their own tools because they tended to take better care of their own property.

A second way to implement the ideas of private property in the workplace is to give clear lines of responsibility. Vague lines of responsibility lead to vague results. How many times has a critical project fallen through because no one individual had the responsibility and authority to see it through. When everybody is responsible, nobody is ultimately responsible.

Companies like Prime Time Shuttle show that Franklin's business legacy is alive and well in America. More than anything else, Franklin has taught us that ownership and rewards pay great dividends in our capitalist economy. Great managers create powerful systems of rewards rather than punishments and penalties. Given this legacy, it's no wonder Franklin ended up on our $100 bill.

What Good Shall I Do This Day?

❑ Use self-interest as a motivator. It may not be the noblest motivator, but it tends to be the most consistent and most effective one.

❑ Use rewards. They tend to be twice as effective as punishments in changing behavior, and the effect lasts twice as long.

❑ Seek to solve organizational problems using interest-based rewards rather than force-based punishments.

❑ Realize you're never as careful managing and spending other people's money.

❑ Avoid rewarding employees simply for exhibiting increased levels of effort. Effort is necessary for higher performance, but it must be properly directed for maximum results.

❑ Establish a link between pay and performance. It is one of a manager's most important jobs.

❑ Use ownership as a base for incentives whenever possible. It's one of the great benefits of working in a capitalist economy.

My being many Years in the Assembly, the Majority of which were constantly Quakers, gave me frequent Opportunities of seeing the Embarrassment given them by their Principle against War, whenever Application was made to them by Order of the Crown to grant Aids for military Purposes. They were unwilling to offend the Government on the one hand, by a direct refusal, and their Friends the Body of Quakers on the other, by a Compliance contrary to their principles. Hence a Variety of Evasions to avoid Complying, and Modes of disguising the Compliance when it became unavoidable. It was in Allusion to this Fact, that when in our Fire Company we feared the Success of our Proposal in favor of the Lottery, & I said to my Friend Mr. Syng, one of our Members, if we fail, let us move the Purchase of a Fire Engine with the Money; the Quakers can have no Objection to that: and then if you nominate me, and I you, as a Committee for that purpose, we will buy a great Gun, which is certainly a "Fire-Engine."

—Benjamin Franklin
on getting the peace-promoting
Quakers to help purchase a cannon

Chapter 9

Doing The Impossible

There are two kinds of pay phones in this world: unlimited talk and timed. In the United States, we are accustomed to unlimited-talk pay phones, which means that we can talk as long as we want on a local call for a flat rate of 35 cents. In Japan, however, it's very different. Japanese pay phones are timed; for the same 35 cents, you may talk only for three minutes on a local call. When your three minutes are up, you have to put more money into the pay phone to keep talking.

In countries that have unlimited-talk pay phones, long calls can substantially reduce the revenue of pay phone companies since phone booths can be occupied for long stretches of time, preventing other potential short callers from using the pay phone. Any obvious method of shortening phone calls or charging more would put a company at a competitive disadvantage relative to other pay-phone providers. Is it possible to shorten phone calls, raise revenues and not start an armed uprising?

Solving The Impossible Problem

As both the opening quotation and the above pay-phone problem demonstrate, one of a manager's most important jobs is to create solutions for seemingly impossible problems. I use the word "create" deliberately. It seems that the price of survival in our ever-changing marketplace is a steady stream of creative solutions. Franklin showed remarkable imagination in creating a way for the peace-loving Quakers to help finance a new cannon.

The Society of Friends, also known as Quakers, was a dominant religious group in Pennsylvania during Franklin's time. One of the Quakers' most distinctive beliefs was their strong stance on pacifism, or avoidance of war. A good Quaker would never bear arms or financially contribute to the purchase of weapons for the common defense. Not surprisingly, this belief was difficult to fully implement in Colonial America, given aggressive stances from American Indians and British and French troops.

Here's the seemingly impossible problem: How do you get money from people to fund much needed defense efforts when their religious beliefs oppose it? Franklin's solution was both reasonable and imaginative. He asked the Quakers to provide funds to help pay for a new fire engine, and they willingly agreed. In turn, the funds were pooled with others to purchase a new cannon—an engine (or machine) that creates great amounts of fire! Best of all, the Quakers could embrace this solution fully aware that the funds were being used for these purposes. They, too, wanted to have some means of defense despite their religious beliefs to the contrary. All Franklin did was create a face-saving mechanism that legitimized the release of Quaker funds into public hands.

Franklin's Ninth Rule Of Management:
Create solutions for
seemingly impossible problems.

So how can a pay-phone provider shorten the average call in a country with unlimited-talk pay phones? One company used a creative approach. They arranged for the manufacturers of the telephone handsets to make them as heavy as possible and still keep the phones functional. After a bit of research, the handset manufactures inserted a large amount of lead into the handset. Obviously, this made the handsets heavier, and callers tired more quickly on longer calls. The idea worked, and the pay phones provided by this company are still heavier than most.

Managing To Do The Impossible

It's easier than you think to do the impossible. This is not some warmed-over motivational talk, either. I simply believe that most people declare as impossible anything that doesn't happen naturally or on a regular basis. This was one of Karl Marx's many problems. Among other things, Marx predicted that capitalism would fail because it

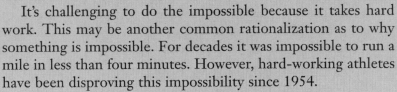

Benjamin Franklin Once Said . . .

"All things are easy to Industry, all things are difficult to Sloth."

It's challenging to do the impossible because it takes hard work. This may be another common rationalization as to why something is impossible. For decades it was impossible to run a mile in less than four minutes. However, hard-working athletes have been disproving this impossibility since 1954.

Lazy (slothful) people are quick to label something as impossible to avoid having to do it. "It's impossible for humans ever to fly," "It's impossible for women to fly," "It's impossible to find a cure for polio," or the more realistic, "It's impossible to double our sales next quarter." Maybe one of the best interview questions you can ask when selecting new workers is, Can you tell me about a time when you did the impossible?

would eventually run out of product ideas and new customer markets. Karl Marx underestimated the ingenuity of management in creating new products and of organizations in producing them. Marx also suspected that capitalism might fail because capital would become concentrated in the hands of an elite few, and the embittered masses would have no means by which to start their own businesses. Once again, he underestimated the creativity of entrepreneurial managers in gaining access to capital through credit cards, family and friends, or just forgoing capital and starting businesses in their garages. Somehow, the idea of e-commerce business start-ups with capital requirements of near zero never crossed Marx's industrial mind, which was occupied with images of large, coal-burning factories.

Management often does the impossible—what other people cannot conceive or expect. The ideas in this chapter get to the very heart of why management exists and is still needed by businesses the world over. If you can master these tasks, you will always be in demand as a manager.

Impossible Achievements

One of a manager's most fundamental tasks is to help people achieve things they never believed possible. A number of novels are part of the required reading in many of my college business classes. These books range from short works like Jack London's *The Call of the Wild* to Ayn Rand's megalithic *Atlas Shrugged*. Students in my four-week summer classes stare at me in disbelief when I tell them that we're going to read Rand's entire 1,100-page novel before the semester ends. Thirty days later, a large majority of students experience the satisfaction of having finished the book—a feat they deemed impossible only a short time earlier.

The technical name I give this management task is "unleashing latent abilities." Latent abilities lie dormant within us, much like a sleeping volcano lies dormant, until somebody cares enough to design a performance system that encourages us to tap into them. Until we tap our latent abilities, we are only shadows of what we might be. Once a great manager taps our latent abilities, we begin to achieve things we once thought impossible.

One of the all-time greatest role models for managers in this area is Anne Sullivan. You probably know her as Helen Keller's teacher.

Nobody in Helen Keller's family or community realized it, but she was a bundle of latent abilities waiting to be tapped. Somehow Anne Sullivan saw the potential and literally fought and wrestled young Helen until she broke through. Almost all of us remember the great scene in the film "The Miracle Worker" when Anne Sullivan and Helen Keller are at the water pump, and Anne yells out, "She knows!" She had broken through into Helen's dark and silent world and would soon unleash a person of uncommon abilities who would eventually lecture to audiences throughout the world.

Our challenge as managers is a little different. Benjamin Franklin looked at his drunken co-workers in the London printing house and could see achievement waiting to be unleashed in the absence of six servings of beer each day. Although it's unlikely that your staff is held back because of drunkenness, all workers should be viewed as only shadows of what they could become if given the proper performance incentives and encouragement. Without good managers, they may never learn that they can do the impossible.

Impossible Differences

Anybody who has ever had formal training in negotiation and bargaining has probably come across the rather infamous negotiation for an orange. This training scenario involves two people who are negotiating with a third party for an orange. The scenario is designed to escalate quickly into a very high-dollar orange purchase unless the two bidders make a startling discovery: They each want the orange for different reasons. One of them needs to use the pulp and juice. The other needs only the rind.

If the two bidders communicate adequately to make this discovery, they stop being enemies who drive the price of the orange skyward in their bidding war and become allies who willingly pool their funds to share the cost of the orange as inexpensively as possible. What at first seemed to be a game of impossible differences becomes a game of differing but complementary interests. Differing but complementary interests are the foundation of every mutually beneficial relationship.

Let me clarify this idea with a few illustrations. The easiest and most obvious example of radical differences forming the foundation of a mutually beneficial relationship is Mars and Venus, or men and women. For centuries, these two very different beings have been forming lasting relationships built solely on differing but complementary interests.

The relationship between business and customer is almost the same. When I purchase gasoline, I'm reminded of this relationship. I commute to work each day, so I'm very interested in transportation. Fortunately, a number of oil companies are also interested enough in transportation to open gas stations in my community. We're inter-

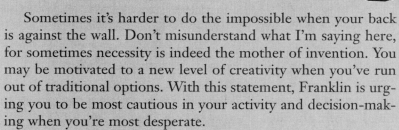

Benjamin Franklin Once Said ...

"Necessity never made a good bargain."

Sometimes it's harder to do the impossible when your back is against the wall. Don't misunderstand what I'm saying here, for sometimes necessity is indeed the mother of invention. You may be motivated to a new level of creativity when you've run out of traditional options. With this statement, Franklin is urging you to be most cautious in your activity and decision-making when you're most desperate.

Desperate people take out loans at higher than normal interest rates. Desperate people buy the first office space they find just to get a roof over their heads. And desperate employers hire the first candidate they see that doesn't foam at the mouth just to get a warm body in the vacant seat. Does Franklin offer a cure for such desperation? Yes. I believe his commitment to frugality offered him relief from the dangers of necessity.

A person or business can eventually accrue a surplus of funds that serve as a guard against desperate decisions. The number-one complaint I hear from entrepreneurs is that they are under-capitalized. They have too much cash tied up in inventory, or their store cost more than they ever imagined when they took out their initial loan. A frugality-driven pool of working capital can liberate you and, best of all, it can be financed from your own pocket.

ested in transportation for different but complementary reasons. I have a car, and they have gas. Thus, we have a basis for exchange.

Business managers should realize that differences are the fuel that drives a capitalist economy. If everyone were the same in a society, we'd have no reason to engage in exchange. The more impossible the difference, the bigger the business opportunity for the manager who is creative enough to discover the complementary interests that often accompany these differences.

Impossible Distances

From its very beginnings, business has been about solving the problems associated with impossible distances. Some of the earliest modern-style businesses in America were the railroads that arose during the mid-1800s. Before the coming of the railroads in America, nobody could fathom the concept of traveling across the American continent in two days or of manufacturing products for a national customer base. Franklin was a visionary businessman by anybody's standard, but he only published his newspaper, *The Pennsylvania Gazette*, for a very local customer base in Philadelphia. Now, it's commonplace for some newspapers to be published for a global customer base.

Business is all about creating ways to overcome the distances that separate people from the products and services they might want. Consider the success of new e-commerce companies like Amazon.com or eBay. eBay's success is founded on the creation of a virtual marketplace where people from around the world can advertise and trade goods. This market used to be limited to the reach of the local want ads—and they weren't interactive. Now, I can advertise my products on eBay and watch buyers in Illinois and Maryland engage in a bidding war to earn my business. What was once an impossible distance between business and customer has vanished.

Now, distance is starting to break down in the traditionally local labor market. E-commerce firms like Monster.com are setting up auction sites in which workers can auction their services to the highest national or even global bidder. Some people may even complete their work and earn their paychecks without ever leaving their own homes as a result of new information and communication technology that allows new levels of telecommuting. Along with impossible achievements and impossible differences, solving the problems associated with impossible differences can be a remarkable business opportunity.

Impossible Social Problems

The laundry list of problems affecting American citizens is long and rather intimidating. I've heard reports of pollution, crime, dead-beat dads, drunk drivers, over-fishing, fraud against senior citizens, and then there's that hole in the ozone layer over Antarctica. In the opening quotation, Franklin and his fellow citizens were faced with the prospect of hostile attacks and were in need of more weapons for defense. Now, I've faced some pretty ugly problems in my time, but hostile attacks take precedence over anything I've faced.

In the spirit of Benjamin Franklin, I want to challenge you to consider social problems not as a justification for government intervention but as a business opportunity. Yes, a business opportunity. I believe that managers hold the keys to organizational systems that are far more effective than government bureaucracies at solving our most pressing social problems. With the power of economic incentives and the competitive demands of the marketplace, managers may be able to provide better solutions than government bureaucracies for some of our most pressing problems. Consider the problem of women in American society who have been stranded with no means of economic support. The bureaucratic solution for this problem has been legislation and welfare programs. The business solution for this problem has been Mary Kay Ash.

Mary Kay Ash is a phenomenal individual by anybody's standard. However, for the thousands of women who have received economic empowerment as a result of her company, Mary Kay Cosmetics, she is approaching divine status. Some claim that she has liberated more women than Gloria Steinem ever did.

Mary Kay was a successful woman stuck in a man's world, and she decided to do something about it. She didn't march on Washington, and she didn't burn her bra. She simply started a company that has produced more women millionaires than any law railroaded through the federal government. Is it possible for a manager to provide a solution for the problem of marginalized women in society? Mary Kay

Safety Net

An impressive example of management providing effective solutions for pressing social problems is the emergence of Internet safeguard services that parents can use to protect their children from potentially dangerous Internet sites and services. Firms like Cyber Patrol, Cybersitter, and Net Nanny quickly emerged in response to the cries of parents to protect their children from pornography, chat rooms that might be unfriendly to children, and other adult-oriented Web-based fare.

History suggests that government regulation lags market reality by a number of years. It might have taken the federal government another five years to pass and enforce legislation that accomplished what these Internet safeguard firms did quickly in response to consumer demand. What many decried as an impossible social problem has proved to be a great business opportunity for many as well as an effective social solution.

Ash's example proves that it is indeed possible. When a social problem exists—marginalized women or homelessness or a deteriorating environment—we typically reach for a governmental solution with shouts of "There ought to be a law." However, managers may be just as effective as bureaucrats in solving pressing social problems.

Benjamin Franklin acted from his experience as a manager to solve a variety of social problems of his day including defense, fire, theft and even the employment of women in his printing businesses and partnerships. All his solutions were implemented without the aid of a federal government simply because no federal government existed. Franklin seemed to make a habit of doing the impossible. He made the impossible rise to international fame from obscure beginnings. He found a way to get the peace-loving Quakers to help buy a new cannon. More impossible still, his example challenges us today.

What Good Shall I Do This Day?

❏ Seek to create face-saving solutions that preserve the true interests of all parties. Sometimes a cannon can be a "fire-engine."

❏ Help your workers set and achieve goals they never dreamed possible.

❏ Follow Anne Sullivan's example and give your workers the gift of a larger life.

❏ Look at differences as your friend. Differing but complementary interests are the foundation of every mutually beneficial business relationship.

❏ Remember, the greater the distance, the bigger the opportunity.

❏ Don't wait for the government to solve our most important social problems. Rather, view them as market opportunities.

When about 16 Years of Age, I happen'd to meet with a Book, written by one Tryon, recommending a Vegetable Diet. I determined to go into it. My Brother being yet unmarried, did not keep House, but boarded himself & his Apprentices in another Family. My refusing to eat Flesh occasioned an Inconveniency, and I was frequently chid for my singularity. I made myself acquainted with Tryon's Manner of preparing some of his Dishes, such as Boiling Potatoes or Rice, making Hasty Pudding, & a few others, and then propos'd to my Brother, that if he would give me Weekly half the Money he paid for my Board I would board myself. He instantly agreed to it, and I presently found that I could save half what he paid me.

—Benjamin Franklin
discussing his experiment with a
vegetarian diet and the outcome

Chapter 10

Experiment!

The yearbook is one of the great rituals in American secondary education. Each year, students eagerly await the collection of photos and text that describe the past school year. Part of the ritual is the signing party where students get together and sign each other's books with sentimental and wildly humorous phrases. Many stock phrases continue to make the rounds at this annual school event. Among the favorites are "Stay sweet!" or "See you next year!" and the classic "You are 2 cool 2 be 4-gotten."

Despite my fond feelings for this ritual, some of the worst advice I ever received was written in my yearbook. In fact, there was advice written in my yearbook that would have proven disastrous on more than one occasion had I heeded it. What was this wretched advice? It was "Don't go changing, and you'll go far!"

I'm sure that this advice was well-meant by the 13-year-old who penned it. Looking back, however, I can definitely say that the quality of my life would be dramatically different if I had followed it. I can unequivocally say that the one thing that has made all the difference between then and now is a willingness on my part to change. Had I chosen to avoid change and remain the same person I was in junior high, I would still be hoeing cotton in the fields of Lamesa, Texas, instead of working as a university professor.

Franklin's Experimental Beginnings

Most of us know about Franklin's willingness to experiment, primarily because of his electricity experiments that involved flying a kite during lightning storms. That one event in Franklin's life should be enough to establish a basis for the discussion that follows, but his attitudes toward curiosity and experimentation go well beyond that single well-known story. In short, Benjamin Franklin was willing to change…and, as a result, he went far.

Franklin's 10th Rule Of Management:
Become a revolutionary for experimentation and change.

Franklin was the model of healthy, proactive adaptation. Numerous anecdotes in his autobiography give testament to his willingness to experiment with new ideas and lifestyles and adopt as habit the positive aspects of the new way of doing things. The quotation on page 146 indicates that Franklin was willing to experiment with a vegetarian lifestyle more than a century before California (state slogan: No Red Meat Allowed) was even admitted to the Union.

This experiment was more than just a dietary change. It was an economic experiment as well. Franklin was indentured to his brother, James, as an apprentice during his first experiment with a vegetarian lifestyle. Franklin approached his brother with a tempting offer. James could stop paying for his younger brother's meals to be prepared by the boarding house in which they lived if he would turn over half of the amount he usually paid to his younger brother. Franklin could get vegetarian meals on his own and still have money for books to continue his self-education efforts.

In addition to the experiments with electricity, vegetarianism and beer drinking (see Chapter 6), Franklin's writings relate numerous personal experiments with civic activities such as lighting streets and

"It's Not Personal; It's Strictly Business."

The interaction between family life and business life is nowhere better depicted than in that American film classic, "The Godfather," the film that gave American culture memorable lines like "Make him an offer he can't refuse" to "It's not personal. It's strictly business." Unlike the men in this film, however, our personal circumstances often influence our business attitudes more than we would care to admit.

Benjamin Franklin was the youngest son and 15th of 17 children. Until just recently in America, most families were very large. A number of reasons explain this change, but one of the most important was mortality rates. In Franklin's day, parents had many children because half of them were expected to die before reaching adulthood. For parents, the more children you had, the better the chance that one or two of them might make something of themselves in the uncertain world of Franklin's day where there were no colleges or careers.

Our modern world of education, vaccines, contraceptives and multiple career options have resulted in dramatically smaller families. Two children are now the norm, and these two children are often handled with great care. If one is lost, it is a tragedy of unspeakable proportions. In contrast, when a child died even a century ago, it was unfortunate but not unexpected. When a child today fails out of college, it's a shame to the family. In Franklin's day, if one child failed, 12 more were in line to try to succeed. At home, we put all our eggs in one or two baskets and take as few risks as possible with them. Could it be that your personal situation is making you less willing to play the odds and experiment at work?

cleaning street gutters. He also writes about the evangelistic fervor with which he convinced others to join him in his experiments. He even convinced one of his first employers, Samuel Keimer, to try a vegetarian lifestyle with him for three months.

Managers seeking to learn experimental attitudes from Franklin's example should heed a few warnings. First, this was not experimentation merely for the sake of experimentation. Franklin's approach at the personal level was not to try anything but rather to try something for a particular reason. Second, many of his experiments had an economic objective. Franklin found personal experimentation to be profitable. He cautions readers of his autobiography and almanacs again and again to be aware of the costs of your personal tastes and personal habits. Franklin realized early on that tastes and lifestyle change over the course of time, and a change of habits should follow.

Third, Franklin's distinctive character is a direct result of his willingness to experiment. Many historians contend that Franklin was the first uniquely American character (or is that celebrity?). It's a fine line between "unique" and "weird." Vegetarianism is unique. Eating only broccoli is weird. Franklin's experimental lifestyle resulted in distinctiveness instead of weirdness primarily because of the discipline imposed by the economic nature of many of his experiments. Don't read this chapter as a call for weirdness in the workplace. It is not. Wise managers will experiment only when the disciplining of the marketplace can keep the "weird" factor in check.

Finally, Franklin's experiments were usually small and designed to test the waters rather than to throw all his assets into one wild idea. His enlightened, scientific mind understood how to design a focused, controlled experiment. He ran a variety of smaller experiments and then generalized the outcomes to larger matters. A manager seeking to follow in his path should do the same, whether the experiments occur at the personal or business level.

Reengineering 200 Years Ago

Reengineering has been a popular buzzword of the 1990s. The reengineering movement appeared when the American competitive landscape was changing dramatically. As a result, many firms for the first time began to reconsider the fundamental nature of their business enterprise and how it related to competitiveness. Many firms began to reorganize and reshuffle the components of their organizations in efforts to improve performance.

Franklin well understood the relationship between form and competitiveness. This is nowhere better illustrated than in his account of a reengineering effort aboard a ship sailing between the American Colonies and London. Franklin's experimental biases resulted not only in his personal experiments but also in observing the experiments of others and learning from them. Although he did not direct the reengineering effort on the ship, his observations led to some basic conclusions about organizational form and competitiveness. Franklin writes,

> "Our captain of the Packet had boasted much before we sail'd of the Swiftness of his Ship. Unfortunately when we came to Sea, she proved the dullest of the 96 Sail, to his no small Mortification. After many Conjectures respecting the Cause, when we were near another Ship almost as dull as ours, which however gain'd upon us, the Captain order'd all hands to come aft and stand as near the Ensign Staff as possible. We were, Passengers included, about forty Persons. While we stood there the Ship mended her Pace, and soon left our Neighbor far behind, which prov'd clearly what our Captain suspected, that she was loaded too much by the Head. The Casks of Water it seems had been all plac'd forward. These he therefore order'd to be remov'd farther aft; on which the Ship recover'd her Character, and prov'd the best Sailer in the Fleet."

This passage is a great example of a "quick and dirty" organizational level experiment. Managers seeking to imitate Franklin can learn how to design meaningful organizational experiments. First, there was conjecture as to the cause of the problem. The captain suspected the ship was too heavy in front and therefore dragged unnecessarily as the wind tried to push her through the water. Therefore, as a test, he asked all passengers on the boat to move to the rear of the vessel. Second, he immediately took key measurements to determine whether any changes in speed occurred. A log line was dropped into the water, and the captain could immediately tell if the ship was gaining or losing speed as a result of the passengers moving to the rear. Finally, the experiment involved changing only one factor: The weight of the passengers was shifted to the rear to bring more balance and get the nose of the ship out of the water. Once the captain determined that too much weight in the front was the cause, he moved all the water casks to the rear of the vessel rather than having the passengers stand in the rear for the remainder of the voyage.

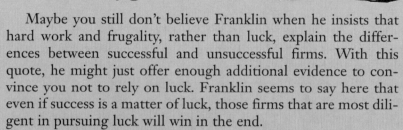

Benjamin Franklin Once Said...

"Diligence is the mother of good luck."

Maybe you still don't believe Franklin when he insists that hard work and frugality, rather than luck, explain the differences between successful and unsuccessful firms. With this quote, he might just offer enough additional evidence to convince you not to rely on luck. Franklin seems to say here that even if success is a matter of luck, those firms that are most diligent in pursuing luck will win in the end.

The experimental mindset discussed in this chapter is the foundation of such diligence-centered quest for luck. If you happen to be dealing with a business scenario where it's a genuine game of probabilities, then experimentation may be your best route to success. For example, in agriculture, crop production is often more a matter of getting the right amount of rain and sunshine and avoiding hail damage. People will say that some farmers were lucky and other weren't, but the fact is that all were subject to random weather fluctuations. As much as we would like to be in control, we just can't exert much influence over weather patterns. However, farmers survive these random weather fluctuations through experimentation and diligence.

First, farmers will experiment with different crops and different locations for growing them. Successful farmers tend to have a variety of land sections scattered widely across the countryside. Second, successful farmers just stay at it. One bad year doesn't make them throw in the towel and apply for the first government job that comes along. Be diligent in your work and diligent in your experimentation. Your adversaries will call you lucky. You will know otherwise.

In reality, one-factor experiments with clearly measurable outcomes might not be possible in complex business environments. Nevertheless, thinking simply but clearly about your workplace experiments may provide the necessary beachhead from which further change efforts can be launched. Managers can make the mistake of trying to make the experiment as real as possible and then throwing up their hands in defeat when no experiment is possible. Worse still, they might design an overly complex experiment from which no clear conclusion can be made because no lines of cause and effect can be drawn.

Whether at sea or on land, Franklin notes in a later passage that good management can make the difference between success and failure.

> "It has been remark'd as an Imperfection in the Art of Ship-building, that it can never be known 'till she is try'd, whether a new Ship will or will not be a good Sailer; for that the Model of a good sailing Ship has been exactly follow'd in the new One, which has prov'd on the contrary remarkably dull. I apprehend this may be partly occasion'd by the different Opinions of Seamen respecting the Modes of lading, rigging & sailing of a Ship. Each has his System. And the same Vessel laden by the Judgement & Orders of one Captain shall sail better or worse than when by the Orders of another."

Franklin is correct in noting that it's not necessarily bad equipment but a bad captain that can make the difference between success and failure. Among other things, bad captains are probably unlikely to experiment with anything new for fear of being wrong. Whether it was a ship at sea or a printing operation, management mattered in Franklin's day, and it matters today.

Becoming A Revolutionary Change Agent

Franklin was no stranger to breaking with tradition and habit at either the personal or institutional level. At the personal level, Franklin offered these words of warning about the power of habit and tradition:

> "Habit took the Advantage of Inattention. Inclination was sometimes too strong for Reason. I concluded at length, that the mere speculative Conviction that it was our Interest to be

completely virtuous, was not sufficient to prevent our Slipping, and that the contrary Habits must be broken and good ones acquired and established, before we can have any steady uniform Rectitude of Conduct."

Franklin knew that our personal habits make us who we are and that these habits gain momentum over time. Bad habits must be identified, broken and replaced by new ways of doing things.

Here's an example of how easily we stop questioning long-held traditions and habit. A mother and daughter were in the kitchen one Christmas cooking the traditional Christmas ham. The mother took pride in giving her daughter the same lesson she received from her own mother a quarter century before. She summed up the morning for her daughter, "So remember, cut off the ends of the ham, put it in the pan, brush on the glaze, and bake."

"Why do we need to cut off the ends, Mommy?" asked the daughter rather innocently. The mother searched her mind and gave the only answer she could find, "Well, honey, I don't know why. That's just how your Grandma taught me." The daughter insisted on knowing the answer so the mother agreed to call Grandma.

"Hello, Mother," she said as Grandma picked up the phone. "Why do we need to cut the ends off the ham before we glaze and bake it?" The phone was silent while the mind on the other end retrieved the necessary information. "Well," said the grandmother, "My baking pan was always too small so I had to cut the ends off the ham or it wouldn't fit in the pan."

Isn't it funny how one generation's rational, efficient solution to a problem becomes the next generation's legitimized but inefficient and irrational tradition? This is not just a culinary phenomenon, either. Business activities are highly susceptible to this disease that could be known as "hardening of the activities." If not questioned, record-keeping and budgeting activities designed for one competitive era end up being competitive liabilities in the next. Staffing practices created in America's industrial heyday, like full-time employee relationships and rambling, hour-long interviews, persist in the Digital Age where leaner organizations are discovering the benefits of self-selecting independent contractors.

Franklin fought this battle not only at the personal level but at the institutional level as well. Revolution was in the air when Franklin returned to the American Colonies from a political trip to England in 1775. Immediately upon arrival, he began working ardently as a revolutionary. Historically, one of his most important tasks was to review working drafts of the Declaration of Independence written by Thomas Jefferson. Franklin eventually signed his name to that document as one of the delegates from Pennsylvania. In doing so, he pledged his life, fortune and sacred honor to the independence effort.

The Declaration of Independence offers a powerful framework for fighting dysfunctional habits and promoting change at the institutional level. Let's take a closer look at the logic of this historic document as it relates to promoting change in dysfunctional organizations.

"We hold these truths to be self-evident, that all men are created equal, that they are endowed by their Creator with certain unalienable Rights, that among these are Life, Liberty and the pursuit of Happiness."

- **People are first.** Governments exist to protect the rights of the individuals creating the government. At least this seemed to be the mind-set of the early American revolutionaries. Their organizational arguments focused on the creation of governments to protect the rights of individuals. Most of their thinking in this area was influenced by Thomas Hobbes' book *Leviathan*, which is a seminal text in explaining and justifying the rise of government in societies.

  Governments, unfortunately, are not economic organizations. The year 1776 is notable not only for the writing of the Declaration of Independence but also for the publication of the first great work of modern economics—Adam Smith's *The Wealth of Nations*. Smith's book provides the theoretical backbone upon which capitalism and its enterprises are built. Unlike Hobbes' *Leviathan*, Smith's book is not concerned with governments and citizens with rights. Rather Smith's legacy is firms and individuals with interests.

  Let's reframe the foundational statements for a business context. Organizations exist to serve the interests of the individuals that comprise the organization. The people make the place, and the people's interests should be central to the design of an effective organization.

> *"That to secure these rights, Governments are instituted among Men, deriving their just powers from the consent of the governed . . ."*

● **Organizations are second.** Organizations are created for the benefit of the people that comprise them. Period. As stated above, an organization is created to protect the interests of the individuals comprising the organization. In the late 1960s, a group of employees at Fairchild Semiconductor believed that their employer was not serving their interests—even though their employer was a prestigious company. As a result, Bob Noyce, Gordon Moore and Andrew Grove left Fairchild Semiconductor to create an organization that better served their interests. That organization was Intel, and the rest is history.

Wherever you find employees excited about going to work everyday, chances are you'll find an organization that is designed to serve the interests of the employees. Interests will vary across individuals as much as appearances. However, common elements include economic interests such as salary, stock and benefits; job interests such as work environment and colleagues; and personal interests such as career goals and leisure activities.

> *". . . That whenever any Form of Government becomes destructive of these ends, it is the Right of the People to alter or to abolish it, and to institute new Government, laying its foundation on such principles and organizing its powers in such form, as to them shall seem most likely to effect their Safety and Happiness."*

● **Organizations become dysfunctional over time.** Your organization is becoming outdated faster than ever before. Sure, we can all grasp the idea of technological change. But change in organizational forms? Why, you can't even see an organizational form. How can something change that can't even be *seen*?

Consider only the changes shaping the employment relationship between Franklin's time and ours. In Franklin's world, there was one kind of entry-level job: apprentice. You worked your apprenticeship as an indentured servant and were promoted to journeyman at the discretion of the master under which you served. After many years as a journeyman, you might be accepted as a master in the guild of your trade.

Today, we no longer have apprentices hoping to become journeymen serving masters in a guild. Since Franklin's time, we have fought a Civil War to eliminate servitude—indentured or otherwise—to any master. We may even be witnessing the twilight of the corporate forms that gave rise to career ladders and unionism. New ways of structuring the traditional benefit-bearing employment relationship are showing up every year. Recent innovations include temporary employees, job sharing, telecommuting and independent contractors or consultants.

Managers must work to identify dysfunctional forms, abolish them and replace them with new organizational forms that serve the interests of the people involved. No organizational routine should be considered sacred. A potential hit list would include compensation design, ownership structure, budget processes, cash flow management, bookkeeping and inventory management to name just a few. Good managers expect dysfunction.

"Prudence, indeed, will dictate that Governments long established should not be changed for light and transient causes . . ."

● **Organizational change is risky.** It's been said (I think it was Groucho Marx) that change is nice but we'd all really prefer whole bills. Unfortunately, those bills are not guaranteed whenever a change effort is instituted. The history of American business is riddled with firms that tried to change and failed. Consider Coca-Cola and its ill-fated New Coke. Consider Continental Airlines' failure trying to copy Southwest Airlines' operational model with Continental Lite. The list goes on.

Therefore, a few words of caution are in order before taking these ideas too far. The law of risk and return also governs change. If change were easy and success guaranteed, everybody would be doing it. Change will always involve the risk of failure. Further, managers seeking to change organizations face both the battle for the change itself and—if they win—the bitterness of the survivors who profited under the old system. Buried interests and issues that emerge months after the change is completed stymie sometimes even successful changes. And it gets worse. Sometimes it's not just the losers who resist the change after the fact. Sometimes it's the people involved and interested in the change itself. Read on in the Declaration of Independence . . .

". . . and accordingly all experience hath shewn, that mankind are more disposed to suffer, while evils are sufferable, than to right themselves by abolishing the forms to which they are accustomed."

● **People resist change.** A recovering alcoholic gave me a great bit of advice almost a decade ago. Joe had been dry for a number of years and had become involved with an organization center that reached out to the working poor and near-homeless in Dallas. As a recovering alcoholic, Joe brought a unique perspective to his work with people teetering on the edge between daily survival and a never-ending downward spiral. When we discussed a particular case at the center, he would often interject, "Well, if nothing changes, nothing changes."

His wisdom gleaned from some hard years of personal experience has stayed with me, and I pass it on to others whenever I can. The Founding Fathers were also keen observers of human nature. Simply put, most people resist change. Further, we'll continue to tolerate suffering, hoping that the problem will magically solve itself. Who among us has rushed straight to the dentist at the first sign of a toothache? No, we wait until the pain is so bad that pulling the tooth without anesthetic sounds more appealing than living any longer with the pain.

One of a manager's most important roles is to be the agent for change in an organization. Some might just call this leadership, but it is so foundational to the modern managerial job description that it is difficult to meaningfully differentiate the two. Even though members of an organization may long for a better life at work, most are still unwilling to pull the trigger on any organizational change.

Many workers who desire change are more likely to leave the organization than promote change within.

Why this tendency to ". . . suffer, while evils are sufferable"? Several reasons come to mind. First, America's bureaucratic legacy from the Industrial Age has left us with a fear of failure. Failure was bad for the Organizational Man's career interests. It was better for

Benjamin Franklin Once Said . . .

"The ancients tell us what is best, but we must learn of the moderns what is fittest."

This quotation suggests that Franklin was aware even in his day that change was an inevitable occurrence in life and business. He was also wise enough to notice that all successful changes are going to be rooted in the past. You see, people tend to be attracted to familiarity and tend to avoid uncertainty. Therefore, you should intentionally design the changes in your business to remind people of the past while pointing them toward the future.

The changes at the Walt Disney Co. since the mid-1980s are a great example of this. At that time, Disney was close to folding, but a new CEO named Michael Eisner came on board and set a path for the future. Disney remained a "Magic Kingdom" as a company but began to boldly advance into previously uncharted waters. Eisner led the Walt Disney Co. into successful retailing ventures, Broadway productions and media acquisitions, and re-energized one of their traditional core businesses: movie-making.

Experimentation and change can quickly digress into a second-rate recycling of the past if you're not careful. The acid test of change is whether the change helps you become a stronger competitor. Disney remains one of the most family-friendly companies in the world and a genuine American icon. However, it didn't have to sacrifice its past to ensure its future. It just learned how to become a "Magic Digital Kingdom."

the man in the gray flannel suit to make no decision than a bad decision. Second, our economic interests can lead us to maintain the status quo rather than risk changing an environment where our job, salary and retirement income appear relatively secure. The faster the rate of technological change, the faster the resistance to change as justified by economic interests.

Too Close For Comfort?

Stay close to the customer" is one of those venerable business maxims rivaled only by "Cash is king" and "Buy low; sell high." However, recent competitive trends suggest that staying too close to your current customer base may be fatal in the long run. Intel CEO Andy Grove refers to this as the "segment zero" phenomenon.

Most firms segment their market into a variety of customer groups. At Intel the customer segmentation model looked like a triangle with more narrow, premium customers at the top and larger, commodity-type customer groups at the bottom (segment 1). The segment zero customer group is so small that they don't warrant attention—especially in contrast to more lucrative, premium customers. Further, a true segment zero seems to have the aura of "bottom fishing." For Intel in the mid-1990s, this was the under-$1,000 computer market. For Big Steel in the 1970s, segment zero was the rebar market. For booksellers in the Digital Age, segment zero was the online book market.

A new segment zero market is not only difficult to spot, but it's difficult to forecast future market growth with any accuracy. Intel now has a policy of deliberately experimenting with a variety of products in a variety of segment zero markets. These experiments led to the introduction of the Celeron chip for the under-$1,000 computer market to keep from "giving away" that segment zero market to a firm that might later grab their premium Pentium market. Grove's lesson is that experimenting with every potential emerging market (and failing in most cases) may be the best path to identifying the next emergent opportunity.

A final reason some organizational members may resist change is the simple comfort of habit and tradition. The Founding Fathers referred to ". . . the forms to which they are accustomed." These forms can be anything from company-owned stores in the age of franchising to traditional benefit-bearing employment relationships in the age of the independent contract. Whatever the forms, they fit some members as comfortably as a slipper, and these people are unwilling to change shoes.

The bad news for those who resist change is that environments are changing more rapidly than ever before. Changing technology, changing regulation and ingenious entrepreneurs are forcing more and more businesses to change or perish. Joe's advice should be nailed on the doors of all who resist change: If nothing changes, nothing changes.

"But when a long train of abuses and usurpations, pursuing invariably the same Object evinces a design to reduce them under absolute Despotism, it is their right, it is their duty, to throw off such Government, and to provide new Guards for their future security."

● **Freedom motivates the revolutionary.** Despite the dangers of change, the reality of retribution and the resistance to change managers encounter, there's one thing that seems so precious that a manager is willing to enter the fray to obtain it. This one thing is freedom. Great managers give freedom to themselves and their workers, and bad managers take it away. Nothing irritated the Founding Fathers more than absolute despotism and taxation without representation, and nothing continues to irritate the children of the original American Revolution more than losing our freedoms within organizations.

A Revolution At Springfield Remanufacturing

Springfield Remanufacturing was in more trouble than even reengineering could solve. They represented one small plant in the enormous International Harvester corporation—hardly worthy of the attention of the corporate executives. Further, their specialty was re-manufacturing broken-down engines and selling them on the engine aftermarket, nobody's idea of a robust market niche. They had one thing going for them, however. His name was Jack Stack, and he was a revolutionary for experimentation and change.

Jack Stack had all the traits of a revolutionary. First, he gave free-dom to his people. Stack and his management team devised a plan to purchase the Springfield Remanufacturing facility from International Harvester for $9 million. They did this through a highly leveraged buyout. Stack and his management team scraped together $100,000, and somehow they convinced a loan officer to lend them the addi-tional $8.9 million—a debt-to-equity ratio of 89 to 1! With this money, Stack and his employees literally purchased their jobs from In-ternational Harvester. Freedom wasn't free, however. The plant now had the freedom to fail, and all could potentially be lost.

The second sure sign that Jack Stack was a revolutionary manager was that he was quick to get rid of dysfunctional organizational forms. He didn't stop, either, with severing the dysfunctional corpo-rate ties through the leveraged buyout. Stack went on to destroy dys-functional hierarchy as characterized by closed-book management. Just as freedom of speech is central to the functioning of a demo-cratic government, freedom of information is central to the func-tioning of a business in a capitalist environment. Stack opened up every management book and management plan for review by the workers who actually rebuilt the engines. Stack's logic was that bet-ter-informed workers would make better decisions in the long run. Furthermore, he suspected that managers would act in a more ac-countable fashion if their decisions were open for public review and critique by the workers.

Finally, Jack Stack was a revolutionary manager because he rebuilt the Springfield Remanufacturing organization around his people. The workers at Springfield Remanufacturing were taught how to read the plant's financial statements and operating reports. This new knowl-edge genuinely empowered them to make better decisions every time they started a new remanufacturing project. The workers were also al-lowed to purchase shares of the company through a stock ownership plan, and a quarterly bonus system was established to share the gains of increased productivity.

Stack's revolutionary insight was building an organization that coupled localized information with powerful incentives. The new Springfield Remanufacturing was a plant where the individuals with the best local information (those who knew how to repair an engine) were given the feedback and incentives to most effectively leverage their choices. The results were nothing short of astounding. Springfield Remanufacturing not only repaid the loan, but equity began to sky-rocket. Over time, the once-doomed plant added a multitude of new employees and even established start-up plants after their own model.

Managers like Jack Stack remind us that America was born out of revolution. As such, there's still a place for revolutionary managers in our economy. Franklin's example of change and experimentation challenges us to create revolutionary businesses. Sometimes this involves experimenting with new products and services at the fringe of the organization. Sometimes it means experimenting with the entire organization as Jack Stack did. Regardless, it means that you had better start experimenting.

What Good Shall I Do This Day?

❏ Experiment with your own life. This will help you be more comfortable with experimentation and failure.

❏ Change is risky, and success is never assured. Therefore, experiment with change efforts when possible.

❏ Remember, experimentation is about becoming a unique individual. Not weird but unique.

❏ Experiment with your organization. Sometimes just moving a few of the pieces around makes all the difference.

❏ Whenever possible, design your experiments with a clearly measurable outcome and only one changing factor. This way, a clear diagnosis of the problem and solution can be made.

❏ Sometimes you need to change the captain instead of changing the ship.

❏ Revolutionary times call for revolutionary actions. Become a revolutionary for change.

❏ Deliberately design your organization to serve the interests of the people involved.

❏ Expect resistance to change.

❏ Great managers give freedom. Poor managers take freedom away.

S ome may think these trifling Matters not worth minding or relating. But when they consider, that tho' Dust blown into the Eyes of a single Person, or into a single Shop on a windy Day, is but of small Importance, yet the great Number of the Instances in a populous City, and its frequent Repetitions give it Weight & Consequence; perhaps they will not censure very severely those who bestow Attention to Affairs of this seemingly low Nature. Human Felicity is produc'd not so much by great Pieces of good Fortune that seldom happen, as by little Advantages that occur every Day.

—Benjamin Franklin
reflecting on the importance of
keeping streets free of dust

Chapter 11

The Importance Of 1,001 Small Details

As a businessperson, you've probably stayed in more hotels than you care to admit. Let's suppose that you're traveling on business and decide to stay at the Great View Inn. Not surprisingly, the Great View Inn is known throughout the United States for having an exceptionally great view. You rationalize the extra money you'll spend at the Great View Inn by telling yourself that you have earned this after all those miles in the car followed by the long meetings.

You arrive at the hotel and are promptly taken to your room by the check-in crew. The luggage attendant lays aside your bags and then throws open the window curtain with a well-rehearsed sweep of his arm. "A room with a view, sir," he announces, and what a view it is! Breathtaking. Stunning. You've never seen anything like it. You tip him, he departs, and you settle down into a chair to enjoy the great view. You decide to call your spouse to share the moment. You have trouble getting an outside line, so you call the hotel operator and ask for assistance.

"I'm sorry," she responds, "but your phone connects only with the front desk. By the way, how's your view?" The view's magnificent, you respond, but this phone thing is a bit odd. Nevertheless, you put the phone aside and decide to unwind a bit with a hot shower. In the bathroom, you not only find that there's no hot water but that the towels are still wet and soiled from the previous guest. You quickly call housekeeping, and they say that they'll get to you if they can, but they will make no promises. "I hope you're enjoying the view," responds the housekeeping manager as you hang up the phone. You probably have figured out by now that the Great View Inn may have a great view, but that's about all.

Franklin believed that the key to human happiness—or human felicity as he calls it in the opening quotation—lies not in the one or two really great moments in our lives. Rather, genuine happiness comes in the hundreds of small details that make up the greater part of our lives. Chances are that the same principle of human happiness applies to business success. The Great View Inn may have had a really great view, but it was not enough to compensate for dozens of irritations that might accompany a stay there. Franklin wisely realized that even small irritations have the potential to snowball and can transform any experience into a miserable time. A little dust in one person's eye may not require civic action to correct. However, when a little dust gets into everybody's eyes several times during the day, you can quickly transform an otherwise livable city into a city of irritated people in perpetually bad moods.

Franklin's 11th Rule Of Management:
Sometimes it's better to do 1,001 small things right than only one large thing right.

The Trouble With One Great Idea

At the end of his life, Franklin had a number of significant accomplishments in a variety of fields. He was a businessman, inventor, statesman, scientist, writer and humorist. Let me make an important point here: Franklin isn't known for just one great idea. He's known for several great ideas. Let's take a moment to contrast Franklin with another important American who was known for just one great idea, Henry Ford.

Almost everybody is familiar with the name Henry Ford, but some are confused about what he invented. Henry Ford did not invent the automobile. Rather, Henry Ford invented the process of mass manufacturing automobiles. Ford was the very first to figure out how to line up all the parts of an automobile along one assembly line and coordinate the activities of hundreds of workers. Mass manufacturing was a great idea, and Henry Ford rightly deserves his place in the pantheon of legendary American managers. Unfortunately, mass manufacturing was Ford's only great idea.

The trouble with one great idea is that it can be easily copied by others. Henry Ford had a huge head start on everybody else. He was able to make more cars and sell them cheaper than any other company for well over a decade. His plants paid higher wages than any others, and he democratized the purchase of automobiles so almost every United States citizen could afford to purchase one. Ford dominated the early automobile industry and ranked as a folk hero, much like Franklin in his day.

In the end, however, other automobile companies were able to imitate Ford's mass manufacturing process. Also, General Motors, under the leadership of Alfred P. Sloan Jr., diversified its product offerings and targeted different priced automobiles to different segments of the American consumer market. Henry Ford's only response was to continue mass manufacturing the same automobile and hope that everybody else was wrong. Put differently, he did the same thing but more fanatically. Sadly enough, Ford never had another really great idea and almost ran the Ford Motor Co. into the ground before he died in 1947.

Don't misunderstand what I'm saying here. Great ideas happen, but they are usually few and far between. Unfortunately, too many

Running Hard At Amazon.com

Seattle-based Amazon.com began with one really great idea: selling books online. As a result, Amazon.com will be known as the first great Internet-based business, even though they still have not turned a profit as of the writing of this book. In the beginning, Amazon.com heralded itself as Earth's Biggest Bookstore, and they were. Web-based shoppers marveled at the selection of books that were available through this one-stop shopping outlet.

The biggest competitive problem in the Digital Age is that good ideas are easier and cheaper than ever before to imitate. It wasn't long before Amazon.com began to see other online bookstores pop up on the Web and threaten to take away some of its business. CEO Jeff Bezos has realized that to make it in the Digital Age you've got to have more than just one big, easily imitated idea.

The company no longer promotes itself as Earth's Biggest Bookstore but rather as Earth's Biggest Selection. Soon after competitors began arriving, Amazon.com diversified its selection to include not only books but also music and videos. When a competitor matched this product mix, Amazon.com added online auctions and e-cards. Recently Amazon.com began selling toys and small electronics. Apparently, the goal is to become a unique, one-stop online shopping experience with a hard-to-duplicate selection of products. With every successful change, Amazon.com becomes less and less of a "one great idea" company.

people use the lack of a really great idea as an excuse for procrastination or inactivity. "I could have been successful, but I never could come up with any really great ideas," they complain as they enviously watch other successful people who moved forward without ever having a great idea. Franklin urges every manager to take action and seek effectiveness in small matters rather than waiting for the bolt of lightning that will probably never strike.

The Benefit Of 1,001 Small Ideas

The trouble with one great idea is that it is easily copied. The good news about 1,001 small details is that they often lead to unique and highly differentiated products and services that are difficult for competitors to imitate. One of the great truths of competitive advantage is things that are hard to imitate are often long-term sources of competitive advantage. A good example of this is the success story of Southwest Airlines.

Southwest Airlines has been profitable every quarter since its founding in 1972. This unprecedented feat is doubly impressive given that they operate in the brutally competitive air transportation industry. So what's the key to their success? Although it's tempting to say the key is high-occupancy, short hops and fast turn-around times, there's really more to it than that. Ultimately, another airline can copy this formula for success. Another tempting answer is to say that they are a low-cost provider. This is true and harder to imitate, but there's still more. Most analysts end up talking about the unique culture at Southwest Airlines.

It's difficult to explain the culture at Southwest Airlines in just a few words. Maybe it's because their employees are encouraged to wear shorts to work and crack as many jokes as possible. Maybe it's the hard-working and fun-loving personality of their founder and CEO Herb Kelleher. Maybe it's the airplanes that are painted to look like killer whales. Maybe it's the flight attendants who hide in the overhead luggage compartments and scare you when you open the door. Maybe it's the jokes you hear when you're waiting on hold to purchase tickets. Maybe it's not one big thing but a combination of 1,001 little things that make up a company culture that continues to be a wellspring of competitive advantage for the most successful airline of modern times.

Go Ahead, Sweat The Small Stuff

A recent bestseller advised us not to "sweat the small stuff." Although this book aims at teaching people how to better manage the stress in their lives, the overall message seems to be that we put unnecessary stress into our lives if we try to manage the 1,001 small details in life and business. In the quotation at the beginning of this

Minding Your P's and Q's

H as anyone ever admonished you to "mind your P's and Q's"? Interestingly enough, this popular saying may have its roots in the printing industry of Franklin's day. Before the advent of word processors and laser printers, a printer produced a document by composing the document letter by letter from a tray of metal type. After setting the type into rows, he would ink the type and then press it onto a sheet of paper to make an image.

The type for the lower-case letters "p" and "q" were easy to confuse with one another because they are mirror images of one another and because they are set in reverse on the metal type plate so they will print forward on the page. As a result, a careless printer could set P's in the place of Q's and vice versa. This would result in mistakes like "pueens" instead of "queens" and "qoqular vote" instead of "popular vote." Therefore, printers were admonished to "mind their P's and Q's."

The phrase would later evolve into a general admonition to be careful about what you're doing rather than worrying about how others are doing. Nevertheless, the story serves as a powerful reminder that—especially in the printing industry—it really pays to do 1,001 small things well.

chapter, Franklin suggests a very different message. He believed that human happiness was not found in the "great Pieces of good Fortune that seldom happen," but rather in the "little Advantages that occur every Day." In other words, the small stuff is the good stuff, according to Franklin.

This theme appears again and again in Franklin's writings. He advises in his *Poor Richard's Almanacs* to "Beware of little expenses, a small leak will sink a great ship," as he was acutely aware of how a few unnecessary expenses spent on a regular basis could add up to a large sum in the end. It other words, it pays to sweat the small stuff when it comes to controlling costs.

Franklin knew that paying attention to small things could do more than just control costs. It can generate revenue, too. Success from the management of 1,001 small details is not a quick-fix strategy, however. It's a management principle that requires great character. This sort of victory is the victory of the gardener who plants seeds, waters and cultivates, and then enjoys a good harvest long after most of the difficult work is completed. Likewise, victory from the management of 1,001 small details is very similar to compounding interest over the long term in financial matters. Assuming that your money will double every five years, an investment of $500 in a market-indexed mutual fund would yield $108,000 in just 40 years.

Franklin was great at this type of management because he understood the underlying principles that lead to long-term success. Franklin never missed the opportunity to do a good deed for a close friend, enemy or complete stranger. He knew that in healthy societies like Colonial America, those small good deeds would often multiply into great outcomes. As a result of this kind of thinking, Franklin

Benjamin Franklin Once Said ...

*"You may delay,
but Time will not."*

Procrastination may be one of the greatest business vices of all time. Procrastination as a business vice most likely began during the period when agriculture dominated the business world, and it continues today. As the competitive pace has increased in recent decades, it's become easier to avoid doing those things that we find disagreeable. As a result, more and more people have gravitated toward the hope of having one big idea save their firm.

A commitment to a strategy of doing 1,001 small things right is a commitment to avoiding procrastination. Doing 1,001 small things right requires one key element for success: time. It simply takes time for such activities to start bearing results. The sooner you plant your 1,001 seeds for success, the sooner the very organic growth process will begin and the sooner you can begin to harvest the benefits.

avoided many of the traps associated with get-rich-quick schemes or promises of a quick fix for long-standing problems.

Sweating The Small Stuff In Selecting Partners

As noted in the introduction, Franklin was most likely the dominant figure in the American printing industry in his day. From his beginnings in Philadelphia, his operations spread throughout the American colonies and even into the West Indies. To stimulate this growth, Franklin carefully managed the details at the beginning of the partnership to plant the seeds for growth and success later on.

Franklin's success with his partnerships can be attributed to a number of factors. First, Franklin carefully selected his partners only after a lengthy period of observation. This period of observation occurred most often in the master-journeyman relationship, but he could also draw from other areas of his life. For example, when one of his partners died unexpectedly, Franklin successfully continued the partnership with the partner's widow—a very progressive arrangement for Colonial times. He also set up a partnership with one of his nephews. In fact, this nephew was the son of the brother from whom Franklin ran away as an apprentice. Franklin believed that this helped, in a small way, to repair the damages done by his breach of indenture contract.

A second key to Franklin's partnership success was that he gave the working partner maximum financial freedom. He wrote in the autobiography,

> "In 1733, I sent one of my Journeymen to Charleston, South Carolina where a Printer was wanting. I furnish'd him with a Press and Letters, on an Agreement of Partnership, by which I was to receive One Third of the Profits, of the business, paying One Third of the Expense."

In setting up a partnership, Franklin apparently furnished the working partner with press and type and helped provide working capital. In return for paying one-third of the partnership's operating expenses, Franklin would receive one-third of the profits. In other words, the working partner was allowed to keep the larger percentage of the fruits of success. Furthermore, Franklin's cut was not a flat rate but rather on a percentage basis, so he, too, could prosper if the business grew.

A third key to Franklin's success with partnerships was his ownership incentive. Later in the autobiography he would say more about his partnerships. He states,

> "The Partnership at Carolina having succeeded, I was encourag'd to engage in others, and to promote several of my Workmen who had behaved well, by establishing them with Printinghouses in different Colonies, on the same Terms with that in Carolina. Most of them did well, being enabled at the End of our Term, Six Years, to purchase the Types of me; and go on working for themselves, by which means several Families were raised."

Apparently, the partnership contract allowed for his partners to purchase the press and type Franklin initially provided at the end of a six-year term. Not only did this allow Franklin a means with which to recoup his initial capital outlay, it also provided a powerful incentive to the working partner: freedom of ownership. In such a situation, a working partner would be motivated to grow the business as much as possible to purchase his freedom in six years and continue a reputable business. Franklin, in contrast, was then well positioned to provide the now independent working partner with the ink, paper and other printing supplies necessary to operate a printing concern. Franklin's involvement in the supply chain would benefit his business interests well beyond the end of the formal partnership.

Finally, Franklin offers one final bit of advice in setting up a partnership. His own words speak most clearly on the matter:

> "Partnerships often finish in Quarrels, but I was happy in this, that mine were all carry'd on and ended amicably; owing I think a good deal to the Precaution of having very explicitly settled in our Articles every thing to be done by or expected from each Partner, so that there was nothing to dispute, which Precaution I would therefore recommend to all who enter into Partnerships, for whatever Esteem Partners may have for & Confidence in each other at the time of the contract, little Jealousies and Disgusts may arise, with Ideas of Inequality in the Care & Burden of the Business, &c. which are attended often with Breach of Friendship & of the Connection, perhaps with Lawsuits and other disagreeable Consequences."

Benjamin Franklin Once Said . . .

"Blessed is he that expects nothing, for he shall never be disappointed."

Do you find yourself constantly struggling with disappointment as a manager? Do you find that the difference between your expectations and reality is consistently running at an emotional deficit, whether it's your firm or your colleagues or yourself? Another problem with the "one big idea" mentality is that it can easily lead to disappointment when that hoped-for idea never materializes. Franklin has a bit of wisdom for you in handling your disappointment: expect nothing. Sounds kind of like something a Zen master might say as he claps his hands in front of your face, doesn't it?

If you find that disappointment is constantly dragging down your performance as a manager, the best strategy is to manage your expectations. This is not to say that you should give up having goals or planning for the future. Any time we think about the future, we are dealing with expectations. However, Franklin suggests that the only place the future really exists is in your mind. If you find that you are constantly overestimating future performance or how customers or partners will act in the future, you should learn to expect nothing.

Here's an example: Let's say you constantly have high hopes for how quickly new employees will learn their jobs. You've noticed that more often than not you find yourself thinking that new employees learn too slowly, and tension develops because of what you perceive as their slowness. Instead of having high hopes, expect nothing. This way, most new employees will exceed your expectations, and you will find that new employees are faster learners than you thought. As a result, you might find yourself praising them for their progress rather than pressuring them to improve faster, thus lessening the tension in the relationship.

Franklin recommends in this passage that there is no substitute for an explicitly worded contract in managing affairs in a partnership. He's not suggesting here that *every* contingency must be spelled out. Rather, he suggests that it's prudent to rely on clearly stated rules for splitting expenses and revenue and to state as precisely as possible the work expectations of all parties involved. He found this preferable to allowing any notion of friendship to govern the allocation of labor and money between two individuals. However rosy and optimistic things may seem at the beginning of a business, petty grievances will arise, and it's beneficial to have an impartial contract governing disputes. Maybe sweating the small stuff helps everybody live a more stress-free life, after all.

All The World's A Stage

Our modern world of business is very different from the simple agricultural economy that characterized Franklin's Colonial America. In their recent book *The Experience Economy*, consultants and frequent *Harvard Business Review* contributors Joseph Pine and James Gilmore contend that our economy has evolved well beyond agriculture and trade. They suggest that the American economy has evolved through three distinct phases: the agricultural economy of Franklin's day, the industrial economy that began after the Civil War, and the service economy that has characterized much of the late 20th century. These authors now believe that America is poised to enter what they call the "experience economy" in which businesses earn money by providing deliberately staged, memorable experiences for customers.

If all this seems a bit unbelievable to you, they urge you to consider the example of the experience economy pioneer: the Walt Disney Co. Disney has been staging and selling memorable experiences to families for decades in its theme parks. Theme restaurants like the Hard Rock Cafe and Planet Hollywood have picked up on this idea and sell memorable dining experiences along with food and drink. Not surprisingly, these authors believe that the key to successfully selling experiences is in managing the 1,001 small details that make up a complete, professionally staged experience.

Lest you think that their ideas are limited to the restaurant, retail or entertainment industries, Pine and Gilmore give examples of what other businesses are doing to provide experiences. Consider British

Airways, which goes beyond selling air travel and has moved toward selling a relaxing and rejuvenating experience for weary business travelers. Second, Standard Parking of Chicago decorates each floor of its parking garages with icons from different Chicago sports franchises. Each floor also has a signature song that is played on that floor. The murals and the music give the customers a unique parking experience, and they help customers remember which floor they've parked on. Finally, there's the Geek Squad from Minneapolis. You've probably already guessed that they are computer installation and repair professionals. Clients remember the costumed "special agents" complete with classic cars, thin black ties and official badges. They transform a routine computer installation into an experience that you tell your friends about.

Pine and Gilmore offer some advice for businesses that want to move beyond services and start selling experiences. First, most great experiences are themed experiences. The gaming industry is the best current example of this trend. Casinos no longer just provide traditional gaming services for customers. Rather, they offer complete experiences revolving around themes such as New York City and ancient Rome. Next, experiences should engage as many of the five senses as possible. Customers at the Hard Rock Cafe taste and smell the food, hear the music, and see and touch the rock memorabilia that decorates the restaurants.

Finally, these authors suggest carefully staging experiences to maximize positive cues and eliminate negative ones. For example, the hosts at the Rainforest Cafe announce "Your adventure is about to begin;" they don't say "Your table is ready." It's a small detail for sure, but it definitely sets the stage for a more memorable experience. Likewise, the Walt Disney Co. has mastered the art of eliminating negative cues in its theme parks. When you visit Disneyland, every view down every street is carefully constructed to eliminate any intrusion from the outside world and convince you that you are really in a magical kingdom. If the business world is becoming a stage, then 1,001 small details matter more than ever.

What Good Shall I Do This Day?

❑ Don't let the day go by without planting some seeds for future successes. Do someone you know a favor. Make a new business contact for no particular reason. Small, good deeds often mature into great returns as time goes by.

❑ Be on the lookout for small expenses that occur again and again. Catching these costs can save you great sums in the long run.

❑ Talk to your employees and find out the small things that irritate them. Most of these things can be easily removed from the workplace, and everybody is happier as a result.

❑ If your business consists of only one good, easily imitable idea, your competitive foundation will quickly erode. Try to build a competitive foundation on 1,001 small details unique to your firm.

❑ Think of your business as a garden plot. What good things can you plant in the ground today that will mature and pay dividends as the years advance?

❑ Selecting business partners and new employees is a great time to pay attention to the details. Carefully structure contracts at the beginning of a relationship to avoid numerous problems as time goes by.

❑ Ask yourself how you can incorporate the idea of selling staged experiences into your current business.

❑ If you start selling experiences, involve as many senses as possible and carefully harmonize the cues to provide the richest experience possible.

To secure my credit and character as a tradesman, I took care not only to be in reality industrious and frugal, but to avoid all appearances of the contrary. I dressed plainly; I was seen at no Places of idle Diversion; I never went out a-fishing or Shooting; a Book, indeed, sometimes debauch'd me from my Work; but that was seldom, snug, & gave no Scandal: and to show that I was not above my Business, I sometimes brought home the Paper I purchas'd at the Stores, thro' the Streets on a Wheelbarrow.

—Benjamin Franklin
discussing some of his methods
for managing his reputation

Chapter 12

A Good Reputation
Is Not An Accident

ost people alive today remember cheering for boxer Rocky Balboa during at least one of the five films in which Sylvester Stallone portrayed the underdog fighter. In the early part of the 20th century, there was another Rocky in the American cultural landscape for whom nobody cheered. This Rocky was John D. Rockefeller. The story of how Rockefeller went from successful business manager to Public Enemy No. 1 revolves mainly around mismanagement of media.

First, the good news: John D. Rockefeller was a very good person by anybody's standard. He was a devout Baptist, attended weekly church services and tithed to the church from his early years. He even taught Sunday school classes on occasion at his home church, the Euclid Avenue Baptist Church in Cleveland, Ohio. Additionally, Rockefeller had all appearances of being a devoted husband and conscientious father.

Second, Rockefeller was an organizational genius. He understood the importance of scale and efficiency long before others of his time. Further, he pioneered the development of the trust—a vertically integrated, multistate organization so powerful that it was ultimately outlawed. Nonetheless, his managerial and organizational genius was at the root of much of the fortune produced by his operations.

Finally, Rockefeller made many others wealthy as well. As a principal of the Standard Oil Company, he was the prime beneficiary of his company's success. Almost all his top managers profited handsomely, too. What's news to most people, however, is that many of Rockefeller's adversaries also benefited from his success with Standard Oil. Rockefeller sought to eliminate competition whenever possible, usually by buying his competitors' interests outright. This may seem like an obvious move, but in its day it was revolutionary. More often than not, when he approached a competitor with a buyout proposition, he gave them the choice of cash or Standard Oil stock. Those competitors wise enough to choose the stock option profited considerably, because the Standard Oil Company increased in value as the industry was consolidated.

However, in contrast to the media-literate Franklin, Rockefeller did very little to manage his public image, nor did he cater to those media outlets that controlled what America would think of Rocky. His views on public opinion can best be summarized in his contention that the public had no rights concerning his private business contracts. One particular member of the public decided that John D. Rockefeller deserved more public scrutiny than he received. Her name was Ida Tarbell.

Ida Tarbell wrote a series of articles in *McClure's* magazine describing the workings of the Standard Oil Trust in intricate detail. Further, she forced the otherwise reclusive Rockefeller to become a public citizen, much to his chagrin. Her articles were the first shots in the battle that resulted in the breakup of the Standard Oil trust years later. The private, yet virtuous, Rockefeller found himself hideously characterized as a penny-pinching vulture who preyed on the public and filled his own coffers with filthy lucre.

Rockefeller's fundamental mistake was his failure to deliberately and proactively influence the public's perception of his reputation and legacy. In his latter years, Rockefeller hired a public relations firm to shoot film footage of him joking and playing golf like a regular fellow or singing with a group of friends. That film was then circulated to the newsreels of the day. Additionally, his previously private charities became more and more public as he established a reputation as a philanthropist instead of a mere tither at church. Nevertheless, the irreparable damage had been done, and Rockefeller is remembered as a robber baron who tried to redeem himself through philanthropy rather than as the brilliant manager who built what may very well be one of the first modern economic organizations.

Franklin's 12th Rule Of Management:
Deliberately cultivate
your reputation and legacy.

Managing Your Reputation
In The Media

Benjamin Franklin was incredibly media savvy by today's standards. This should come as no surprise now that you know he made his money as a printer, and printing dominated the media of Colonial America. Another of his lucrative business ventures was publishing a newspaper called *The Pennsylvania Gazette*. It was considered to be one of the most successful newspapers of its day, and it is still admired by historians as a model of content, style and overall character.

Franklin deliberately used his media access to influence both his business results and to cultivate his own legacy. He recounts in the autobiography about a time when he used his media channels to generate additional printing business:

> "Our debates possess'd me so fully of the Subject [of a paper currency], that I wrote and printed an anonymous Pamphlet on it, entitled, "The Nature & Necessity of a Paper Cur-

rency". It was well receiv'd by the common People in general; but the Rich Men dislik'd it' for it increas'd and strengthen'd the Clamor for more Money; and they happening to have no Writers among them that were able to answer it, their Opposition slacken'd, & the Point was carried by a Majority in the House. My Friends there, who conceiv'd I had been of some Service, thought fit to reward me, by employing me in printing the Money, a very profitable Job, and a great Help to me."

Franklin's success in influencing public opinion for his benefit can certainly be attributed to his literacy and excellence in printing. However, he points out that his adversaries lacked both the ability to write and the ability to publish materials that might carry opposing positions. Through experiences such as these, Franklin learned very early the benefits of deliberately using the media to promote your agendas.

Franklin's media influence was not limited to *The Pennsylvania Gazette* or anonymous pamphlets. A few years later, he began publishing *Poor Richard's Almanac*, which introduced him to the rural population that didn't read newspapers. Further, he reinforced his reputation for all time by writing his own life story in *The Autobiography of Benjamin Franklin*. Not all American managers would fare so well with the media. In fact, Franklin is the exception rather than the rule when it comes to effective media management. John D. Rockefeller's trouble with the media serves as a useful contrast to Franklin's successful media management.

Modern managers can learn a great deal from Franklin's media savvy. First, you should take a proactive stance toward managing your reputation in the media. Although we all can't own newspapers, more of us can employ the services of a good public relations firm to generate positive press to build goodwill for our firms. Otherwise, the first story about you in the local (or national) papers might likely be a negative one. Second, more and more high-profile business managers are publishing their own biographies. For example, Michael Dell just published his life story, *Direct From Dell*. This is a good move for two reasons. First, it lets Dell tell his story in his own words. Second, since his is the first Dell biography, there's the possibility that it might preempt another less favorable biography from being published.

Managing Your Reputation
In The Marketplace

Franklin not only managed his reputation in the media, but he also took great pains to manage his reputation in the marketplace. The opening quotation from his autobiography introduces a few of his methods. Franklin deliberately chose to avoid places of idle diversion like gambling halls or taverns because he didn't want anyone to think that he was a regular participant in such activities. Likewise, he consciously chose to dress plainly, probably because he believed it gave him more credibility with the "man on the street." I also think he wanted to avoid the appearance of having excess profits to spend on lavish living and fine clothing—even if he really had such money. Franklin began to see a connection between his reputation for hard work and his ability to generate new business.

> "It was often 11 at Night and sometimes later, before I had finish'd my Distribution for the next days Work: For the little Jobs sent in by our other Friends now & then put us back. But so determin'd I was to continue doing a Sheet a Day of the Folio, that one Night when having impos'd my Forms, I thought my Day's Work over, one of them by accident was broken and two Pages reduc'd to Pie, I immediately distributed & compos'd it over again before I went to bed. And this Industry visible to our Neighbors began to give us Character and Credit; particularly I was told, that mention being made of the new Printing Office at the Merchants every-night-Club, the general Opinion was that it must fail, there being already two Printers in the Place, Keimer & Bradford; but Doctor Baird . . . gave a contrary Opinion; for the Industry of that Franklin, says he, is superior to any thing I ever saw of the kind: I see him still at work when I go home from Club; and he is at Work again before his Neighbors are out of bed. This struck the rest; and we soon after had Offers from one of them to supply us with Stationery."

Franklin once again was being noticed for his penchant for hard work. The Merchants' Every-Night-Club mentioned in the passage was an association of successful Philadelphia businessmen who met nightly in a private club to discuss the city's current business. The night when the local printing industry was the subject of conversation, the general opinion was that Franklin's new printing business would fail since there were already two established printing houses—Mr. Bradford's and Franklin's former employer, Samuel Keimer.

A member of the club named Dr. Baird came to Franklin's defense, however. He told the others that Franklin's light was burning in his printing house every night when Dr. Baird returned home from the club meeting. Further, he noticed that Franklin began work in the morning earlier than his competitors. This made such an impression on all the other club members that one of them decided to start soliciting business from the young Franklin. With his reputation secured in the established business community, Franklin was on his way. Keimer, on the other hand, did not fare as well, as Franklin notes in this passage:

> "Thus being esteem'd an industrious thriving young Man, and paying duly for what I bought, the Merchants who imported Stationery solicited my Custom, others propos'd supplying me with Books, & I went on swimmingly. In the mean time Keimer's Credit and Business declining daily, he was at last forc'd to sell his Printinghouse to satisfy his Creditors. He went to Barbados, & there lived some Years, in very poor Circumstances."

Franklin notes that Keimer's managerial effectiveness and creditworthiness were closely tied to one another. He had more to say in his autobiography about the importance of taking care of your debts.

The Importance Of Paying Your Dues

One of the main business trends of the 1980s was the return of debt. Michael Milken created the junk bond market, and a wave of debt-financed restructurings swept America. Big business was not the only beneficiary of the rediscovery of debt. Consumers then and now have increasingly used short-term loans and credit cards. Pundits were quick to claim that this widespread use of debt was a terrible tragedy. These naysayers really never offered a solid reason for those claims other than that debt is bad.

In the Colonial America of Franklin's lifetime, debt was more prevalent as a means of financing and exchange than it is today in our seemingly "debt drenched" society. In Franklin's day, there was no common paper currency primarily because there was no central government to issue the money. Most cash that did exist was based on the British system of pounds and shillings. Debt is not bad, in and of itself. Unpaid debts, however, can be disastrous to the debtor and to society as a whole. One of Franklin's fundamental beliefs was the importance of paying your creditors. Observe this principle in the passage below, in which Franklin applauds the character of a close acquaintance he made during his years in London, Thomas Denham:

> "I must record one Trait of this good Man's Character. He had formerly been in Business at Bristol, but fail'd in Debt to a Number of People, compounded and went to America. There, by a close Application to Business as a Merchant, he acquir'd a plentiful Fortune in a few Years. Returning to England in the Ship with me, He invited his old Creditors to an Entertainment, at which he thank'd them for the easy Composition they had favor'd him with, & when they expected nothing but the Treat, every Man at the first Remove, found under his Plate an Order on a Banker for the full Amount of the unpaid Remainder with Interest."

Here Franklin tells the story of a man who failed in business while living in England. Denham had financed his business through debt so he compounded his debt—or paid off what he could to his creditors—and left for America. Denham seemed to have learned a few lessons about running a business as a result of the failure, and he experienced great success in America. Although most people in Denham's shoes would have returned to England to flaunt their new wealth, Denham returned with a different plan. He threw a party for his former creditors under the pretense of thanking them for the favorable terms under which each of them released his debt obligation (the easy Composition). When the plates from the first course of dinner were removed, however, each of them found under his plate a money order for the forgiven debt plus interest.

In the strict legal sense, Denham owed nothing to his former creditors. The creditors had assumed the risk of financing Denham and were compensated for that risk with a higher rate of interest. The creditors had made the choice to write off the bad loans and collect what they could from Denham before he publicly declared that he would leave for America. Still, Franklin suggests here that Denham exhibited something of fundamental importance: the idea that paying your debts not only benefits your reputation but restores society's faith in the credit system as well.

The Importance Of A Legacy

A few decades back, a sociological survey asked the following question to a large number of people 95 years of age and older: "If you could live your life over again, what would you do differently?" The top three answers were quite interesting. First, these near-centenarians said "We would risk more." An interesting comment considering that everyone in the survey sample had survived two world wars and the Great Depression. Second, these seniors said, "We would reflect more," meaning that they would take time to stop and think deeply about their lives and their place in this life. Lastly, they said, "We would do more things that would live on after we are dead." Risk, reflection and legacy—three wishes for a life to live over.

The remainder of this chapter addresses the final wish on the list: legacy. Franklin's 12th Rule of Management challenges us to deliberately cultivate our reputation *and* legacy. Your reputation is what people think about you while you're alive. Your legacy is what people think about you after you're dead. Franklin's desire for a legacy started early. In fact, he carefully planned and cultivated his legacy beginning after his retirement from business. Great legacies like Franklin's are rarely accidental. They are deliberately cultivated and self-sustaining.

A Legacy Of Philanthropy

Benjamin Franklin began a legacy of philanthropy that has become an unspoken expectation of becoming a successful American manager. Franklin's most notable philanthropic contributions were two $5,000 nest eggs, which he bequeathed to the cities of Boston and Philadelphia with instructions that the cities not touch the money for 100 years. By the end of the first 100 years, the funds had grown to almost $400,000 for Boston and about $150,000 for Philadelphia. Each fund eventually endowed important educational institutions in both cities.

In the next century, Andrew Carnegie and John D. Rockefeller established a pattern of philanthropy for all American businesspeople who followed them. Carnegie's sentiment was that he who dies rich dies disgraced. Before his death, Carnegie gave away almost all his money to a wide variety of institutions including universities, peace organizations and public libraries. Similarly, Rockefeller's philanthropy included endowments to the University of Chicago and to Spelman College, the nation's first college for African-American women.

Benjamin Franklin Once Said . . .

"Great Alms-giving lessens no Man's Living."

Why might Benjamin Franklin believe that giving away your money would not lessen your living? I mean, we're dealing with Mr. Frugality here. I suspect that much of Franklin's thinking on these matters is probably rooted in his desire for a very limited, centralized government.

Franklin spoke of almsgiving, so let's focus on how societies handle their problems of poverty. One way to help the poor is through local charities funded by local individuals. A second solution is federal programs funded by federal tax dollars. Needless to say, America is currently experiencing the latter of the two solutions. The poor must be helped, and Franklin suggests helping them through your own charities rather than having government do it through higher taxes.

The frugal Franklin may have had enough foresight to realize that local charities funded by individual almsgiving is cheaper in the long run than federal programs funded by tax dollars. Further, local charities funded with local dollars will have more accountability and, therefore, be more effective than their Washington-based counterparts. It's not a perfect world, and the poor, parentless children and the mentally disabled will be with us forever. Franklin suggests that your own initiative and solutions will be cheaper and more effective in the long run than those of a bureaucrat. As such, voluntary benevolence may keep your tax base lower in the end.

All eyes are upon the current crop of successful American managers as their fortunes continue to escalate. Cable television visionary Ted Turner fired the first shot a few years ago with a $1 billion gift to the United Nations. Bill Gates recently established the Gates Foundation, dedicated to global health and learning initiatives, with total assets of $17.1 billion. Most likely, additional major gifts will come later. Regardless, all Americans have benefited from the legacy of philanthropy begun by Franklin and continued to this day.

Franklin's Legacy Of Smaller Government

During his politically active latter years, Franklin seemed to make a priority of establishing self-governing institutions to provide for the needs of the citizenry rather than allow government to do it. Franklin realized that a nation's government would grow to the extent that its citizenry would allow. Nature seems to abhor a vacuum, and Franklin realized that government would be quick to fill any empty spaces it could and extract more taxes from its populace to fund these additional activities.

Franklin established a variety of privately organized and privately funded schools for the further education of anybody wishing to attend. Aside from his own private education society, the Junto, he established several schools and the University of Pennsylvania. Franklin established privately operated fire companies long before the public (and tax-funded) fire department came on the scene. Also, Franklin established a privately funded library and a privately funded hospital before the government had a chance to do so. Such needs will exist: health, education and fire prevention; and organizations will arise to meet them. The question is, Will these organizations be privately organized nonprofit institutions or government-directed, tax-funded activities?

Benjamin Franklin began his life in obscurity, and when it was over he was known the world over. Part of his fame is due to the fact that he was a remarkable individual. However, other equally remarkable individuals who lived during 18th century America are less well known. The difference might be that Franklin carefully cultivated his reputation and legacy throughout his life. In the end, all you have is your reputation—and Franklin's continues to impress to this day.

Benjamin Franklin Once Said ...

"Liberality is not giving much but wisely."

OK, this sounds more like the frugal Franklin we've come to know and love. Here, he again advocates personal charity. The goal here seems to be not the greatest amount given but best leveraging the money that you do give. I think Franklin believed that we would all benefit by the marriage of business wisdom to personal charity.

The legacy of Franklin and other American philanthropists who have followed his example suggests a few ways that you can maximize the effectiveness of your charitable giving. First, you need to focus your vision on a particular problem or need. Franklin considered it wise to give with a particular end in mind rather than throw your money scattershot across societal problems, hoping that something wonderful happens. John D. Rockefeller once gave money not to eliminate disease but to eradicate hookworm disease in the American South. As a result of his specific vision, hookworm was virtually eliminated in the South within five years of his initial efforts.

Second, set a budget for your charitable contributions. This will give you the freedom to give, knowing that the money is set aside. A charity budget actually empowers you to take better control of your giving by knowing exactly how much you have available to give. Third, be proactive in choosing or establishing your charities. Try to avoid emotionally based appeals—however genuine—that come your way. You'll be much more involved in those you choose for your own personal interests as opposed to those that you get talked into supporting. Finally, since it's your money, make it a priority, hold the people involved accountable and expect results. Although you can't expect the same results as in a business environment, the overall result will most likely improve.

What Good Shall I Do This Day?

❏ Influence what other people think about you by deliberately managing your reputation.

❏ In the absence of any information about you, people will assume the worst. Don't give them that chance.

❏ Pay your debts. It will be one of the most important things you can do to manage your reputation. It's the one place where your private choices are very visible.

❏ If you're a hard worker, find subtle ways to let the world in on the secret. Keep your light lit at night, and push your wheelbarrow through the streets.

❏ You must manage your reputation in the media. Develop a deliberate strategy for doing so.

❏ Business can make the world an even better place through well-directed charitable donations. Develop a focus and plan for your philanthropic activity.

Having emerg'd from the Poverty & Obscurity in which I was born & bred, to a State of Affluence & some Degree of Reputation in the World, and having gone so far thro' Life with a considerable Share of Felicity, the conducing Means I made use of, which, with the Blessing of God, so well succeeded, my Posterity may like to know, as they may find some of them suitable to their own Situations, & therefore fit to be imitated.

—Benjamin Franklin
discussing his purpose for
writing his autobiography

Conclusion
Becoming A Franklin-Inspired Manager

ranklin wrote his autobiography as a series of letters to his son, William Franklin. As he approached the end of his rather remarkable life, Franklin assumed his posterity might like to know how he had achieved such great success, since his rise was so high and his beginnings so obscure. As Franklin states in the preceding passage, it was his hope that his children and grandchildren might find themselves in a similar situation and choose to imitate his effective methods.

I don't know whether Franklin believed that people well outside of his line of descent would be reading his life stories more than 200 years later. Regardless, a great deal has changed in the American situation over the past two centuries. Franklin's life is but one example of great management principles at work, and his solutions to management problems should be understood in the context of the Colonial business environment in which they occurred. Any attempt to imitate Franklin directly will result in one certain outcome: You will become a second-rate Benjamin Franklin. My goal in writing this book is not to nurture thousands of second-rate Benjamin Franklins. My goal is to nurture thousands of first-rate managers who find Franklin's life to be an inspirational source of management activities. Think of these 12 management rules as a compass to guide you whenever you are faced with difficult managerial choices. Further, consider reading *The Autobiography of Benjamin Franklin* in its entirety. You may find that it's a wellspring of inspirational business ideas. Therefore, one last rule is needed before we close the book on Franklin's life as a businessman.

McCormick's First Rule of Reading:
Seek inspiration rather than imitation.

This book offers principles to guide actions as opposed to a prescription for every situation you will face as a manager. Principles provide us with a compass to direct our activities in more effective ways. This book will be useless unless you choose to actively engage the material it contains and let it reshape your management activities.

The Colonial Context

For those readers who remain unconvinced by what I said in the previous paragraphs, allow me to give you some idea of just how difficult it might be to directly imitate Franklin's life in our current world. Let me shed some light on the Colonial environment in which Franklin lived and point out some important differences between then and now.

- **A Transportation Revolution:** The invention of the steam engine in the early 1800s revolutionized transportation. Prior to the invention of the steam engine, mobility was powered by either wind (sailboats), water currents (river barges), animals (horse and carriage) or humans (walking). In the autobiography, we observe Franklin walking, rowing, riding and sailing, but we never see him on a steam-powered boat or train. This is because that technology did not exist.

    The invention of the steam engine had vast ramifications for business. Steam-powered railroads revolutionized business in America and made almost every other form of transportation obsolete. But there's even another revolution between Franklin's time and ours. This second revolution occurred with the invention of the airplane in the early 1900s.

    To imitate Franklin, a modern manager would have to forgo the benefits of modern ground and air transportation, choosing instead to walk, gallop, row or sail to all important business functions. However, a manager inspired by the life of Franklin would understand that time is money and that superior forms of transportation should be used whenever possible. Do you see the difference between imitation and inspiration yet?

- **An Electrical Revolution:** A lot has happened in the past 100 years, and most of it plugs into walls. Electricity as a method of supplying power is barely a century old. In Franklin's time, the scientific effort to understand and harness electricity for popular uses was just beginning. In fact, Franklin and his kite experiments during electrical storms proved to be a valuable contribution to the field of electrical studies.

A manager seeking to imitate Franklin's life would still fly kites in hopes of duplicating the success of Franklin's experiments. To me, this seems a bit like dressing up like Union and Rebel soldiers and reenacting famous battles from the Civil War. It might be great fun on the weekends, but it will probably do very little to enhance your firm's competitiveness. Managers inspired by Franklin's life, however, would be willing to experiment with emergent energy forms to solve their firms' power supply problems. Furthermore, Franklin-inspired managers would investigate other cutting-edge scientific endeavors like biotechnology or materials science, being always on the lookout for useful business applications.

- **A Communication And Information Revolution:** In Franklin's time, all personal communications were conducted by hand-written letters or face-to-face communication. In the autobiography, we see Franklin writing and carrying letters for himself and others. In addition, we see him walking around town from home to meeting hall to conduct a wide variety of face-to-face meetings with people.

  Modern managers wishing to imitate Franklin would need to hand-write all their personal correspondence and speak to other business contacts only in face-to-face meetings. Although personal meetings and hand-written notes might help you cultivate familiarity in business relationships, as a competitive policy they leave much to be desired. Mangers inspired by Franklin would seek to communicate as effectively as possible. This opens up possibilities for all our modern communication technologies including cell phones, pagers, video conferencing, e-mail and forms yet to be invented.

  Franklin-inspired managers also are not limited to newspapers and billboards as forms of mass communication. Along with town hall meetings, these were the dominant media forms in Colonial times. Franklin-inspired managers seek to experiment with new and developing mass communication outlets such as radio, television and the World Wide Web.

- **A Commercial Revolution:** Colonial America was a nation of shopkeepers and tradesmen. Almost all business was done on credit as paper currency, financial institutions and price systems were still in developmental stages. In addition, bartering ruled the day, and nothing even approaching "suggested retail price" existed.

Anybody seeking to imitate Franklin's business practices would be limited to setting up shop in nonair-conditioned, candlelit buildings and ordering most of their supplies from the commercial center of the day—London, England. Someone seeking inspiration from Franklin's life would never be afraid of simple beginnings. Such managers will not hesitate to open a business in a non–air-conditioned building but will seek to improve on their simple beginnings as Franklin did.

Romancing The Business

Which do you find more romantic: candlelight or a halogen lamp? A hand-written letter or a voice mail? A plane ride or a horseback ride? Most people would answer that they find candlelight, handwritten letters and horseback rides far more romantic than halogen lamps, voice mail, or plane rides. Why is this so?

It all boils down to wasted money and wasted time. OK, let's be a little more sensitive: extra money and extra time. Thomas Edison spoke prophetically when he launched the electric revolution in America by stating that he would make electricity so cheap that only the rich could afford candles. It's actually more expensive to light a room with candlelight than with electricity. Likewise, it's more time consuming to hand-write a letter than it is to leave a voice-mail message.

Extra money and extra time signal to our significant others that we care so much that we're willing to break the budget to impress them. Although this might be good policy in our personal lives, it must be used carefully in our business lives. It's probably a good idea to spend extra time and money on important business relationships with suppliers or customers. However, it's probably bad policy to avoid any and all technological progress for the sake of signaling to everybody that you've got the time and money to waste on older, less competitive technologies like telegraphs and steam engines.

- **The American Revolution:** Probably the most profound revolution since Franklin's time is the American Revolution. We operate in a mature capitalist economy characterized by limited government regulation and intervention and sophisticated financial markets. In contrast, Franklin and his contemporaries operated in a crude capitalist environment that still bordered on mercantilism, the dominant economic model for several centuries preceding Franklin's time. Furthermore, Franklin began his business activities as a Colonial subject governed by the British monarchy. We can't even seek to imitate that environment, as it's long since passed. However, Franklin-inspired managers are American revolutionaries every day seeking to promote business, improve the common welfare and limit government intervention.

Benchmarking: Recipe For Mediocrity

Here's one more lesson as you seek inspiration rather than imitation. One of the fastest ways to ensure a complete lack of competitive advantage in your firm is to commit yourself to a policy of benchmarking. Benchmarking, sometimes known as "best practices," is an imitative strategy that sources-out successful practices from successful firms and seeks to implement these same practices in your firm. For example, if a competitor begins using a new manufacturing process, and word gets out about the specific practice, a firm committed to benchmarking would adopt this same practice in its firm as soon as possible.

The problem I have with benchmarking is that it is an imitative strategy at heart. It may have a limited use in keeping some discretionary costs in check (see Chapter 5) but, in the end, a firm committed to benchmarking can never be differentiated from its competitors. In other words, it has no unique source of competitive advantage. Taken to the extreme, all firms and all products and services would be alike in a world of benchmarking.

Don't get me wrong; it's probably a good idea to find out about our competitors' best practices. However, I recommend seeking creative inspiration from these practices rather than settling for bland imitation. Learn about the new practice, digest it and then shape it into something unique to your firm rather than settle for being a second-rate copy of somebody else. Better yet, collect as many best practices as possible, let them all ferment inside your firm, and challenge your team to reassemble the pieces in a unique way designed to gain a new source of competitive advantage.

Here Endeth The Lesson

So here we are at the end of a short book about a rather remarkable businessman. I hope it's been useful reading for you. Franklin's life offers powerful lessons in management for those seeking guidance in their business. If it did not, I would not have wasted all this time writing it, and you would not have wasted your time reading it. You've seen Franklin mostly at his best and sometimes when he stumbled. Avoid the temptation to canonize Franklin as the patron saint of American business. Rather, allow him to be human and let his humanity inspire you toward becoming a better businessperson.

Index

A

AAAA, 78–79
Adaptation, importance of, 28
Air transportation industry, 171
Amazon.com, 141, 170
American Association of
    Advertising Agencies
    (AAAA), 78–79
American Revolution, 199
Angoff, Charles, 62–63
Apple Computer, 57
The Art of Virtue, 102, 104, 111
Ash, Mary Kay, 7–8, 126, 142–143
Authority, respect for, 40
Automobile industry, 59, 62, 169
Axelrod, Robert, 48–51

B

Bald eagle, 75
Beginnings
    Benjamin Franklin's, 2–5
    improving upon, 1–2
    of other business leaders, 5–10
Behaviorism, 128
Benchmarking, 199–200
Ben Franklin stores, 70–71
Berkshire Hathaway, xx, 90
Best practices, 199–200
Bezos, Jeff, 170
BHAG, 110
Birth, prison of, 11
Board games, learning from, 20–22
British Airways, 177–178
Buffet, Warren, xx, 90
Built to Last (Collins and Porras),
    110
Burnout, avoiding, 21
Burr, Don, 28–29, 39, 63

Businesses. *See also* Organizations
    keys to survival of, 28
    metric-driven, 109
    promoting self-education,
        28–30
Business leaders. *See also* Individual
    leaders
    beginnings of, 5–10
    self-education of, 18–20
Business vocabulary, 58
Butler brothers, 70

C

Carnegie, Andrew, xv, xviii–xix, 6,
    188–189
Carnegie, Dale, 56
Carnegie Steel Co., 6
Catallaxy, 58
Caution, 22, 49
Change
    promoting, in dysfunctional
        organizations, 155–161
    resistance to, 158–161
    risky nature of, 157–158
Character Ethic, xix
Charitable giving, 189, 191. *See also*
    Philanthropy
Chess, 21–22
Circumspection, 22
Circumstance, prison of, 11
Clubs, mutual improvement. *See*
    Junto
Coca-Cola Co., 59, 74, 157
Collins, Jim, 110
Collins (friend), 32, 36
Colonial America, 196–199
Commissions, 125–126

Communication, personal, 72–74, 197, 198
Competition
    computer-based experiment on, 48–51
    disadvantages of, 22, 38–39, 48
    learning from, 22
    partnering vs., 57–58
Competitive Advantage (Porter), 57
Competitive Strategy (Porter), 57
Computer industry, 57, 160
Conflict resolution, 51–56
Consultants, 89
Continental Airlines, 157
Cooperation, importance of, 51
Costs
    controlling discretionary, 78–79
    luxurious, 82
Covey, Stephen R., xix
Criticism, preparation for, 109–111
Customer segmentation, 160

D

Debt, 186–188
Deception
    as business strategy, 93
    clarity vs., 51
    self-, 29
Decision-making
    emotionally centered, 92–94
    habits and, 94
    necessity and, 140
    peers and, 94
    with reason, 86–87
Declaration of Independence, 155, 158
Dell, Michael, 8–10, 184
Dell Computer, 8–10, 109
Denham, Thomas, 187
Desperation, 140

Details
    importance of, 167–168, 171–174
    one great idea vs., 169–171
Differences, radical, 139–141
Disappointment, 176
Discourse, 19
Disney, Walt, 6–7, 81
Distance, overcoming, 141–142
Domino's Pizza, 20
Drinking, 87–88, 90, 92

E

eBay, 141
E-commerce, 141–142
Edison, Thomas, 198
Education. See Learning, lifelong
Effort
    link between performance and, 124
    rewarding, 125
Eisner, Michael, 159
Employees
    job satisfaction of, 68–70, 122
    motivation of, 121–124
    productivity of, 69–70
    self-education and, 28–30
    self-managing, 39–42
Enemies
    difficulties identifying, 57
    feedback from, 58–60
    loving your, 56–60
The Enlightenment, 87
Error, prison of, 12–13
The Evolution of Cooperation (Axelrod), 48
Example, importance of, 34–35
Expectations, 176
The Experience Economy (Pine and Gilmore), 177–178
Experimentation, 13, 148–153

F

Failures
  learning from, 63
  preparation for, 108–109
  successful, 74
Fairchild Semiconductor, 156
Family life, 149
Favors, requesting, 60–62
Feedback
  from customers, 109
  from enemies, 58–60
  on values, 108
Ford, Henry, 62, 64, 169
Ford Motor Co., 169
Foresight, 22
Forgiveness, 50
The Founding Fathers on Leadership
      (Phillips), xxiii
Franklin, Benjamin
  as apprentice, xvii, 3–4, 91
  The Art of Virtue, 102, 104, 111
  autobiography of, xvi–xvii, xix,
      56, 62, 184, 194, 195
  on the bald eagle, 75
  bias for action of, 4
  board games and, 20–22
  as business manager, xv
  Colonial environment of,
      196–199
  creed and list of virtues, 105,
      106–107
  critics of, 62–64, 110–116
  death and burial of, xviii, 116
  education of, 5, 12, 16, 20, 21
  experiments of, xvii, 13, 87,
      148–150
  grammar and spelling of, xxiii
  invents bifocals, 94
  Junto and, 23–25
  legacies of, xviii–xx, 188, 190
  overview of life, xv–xviii

The Pennsylvania Gazette, 183
  as political figure, xvii–xviii
  Poor Richard's Almanac, 36, 64,
      111, 184
  as printer, xvii, 43, 87–88, 90, 92
  religious views of, 57
  on the Socratic method, 51,
      55–56
  swimming and, 36–38
  towns named after, 27
  as a vegetarian, 84, 146,
      148–149, 150
  will of, xvi
  as youngest son, 2–3, 11
Franklin, James, xvii, 3–4
Franklin, Josiah, xvii, 3
Franklin, Massachusetts, 27
Franklin, William, 195
Freedom, motivation of, 161
Frugality
  as disaster insurance, 79
  industry and, 70–71
  luxury vs., 82
  modern examples of, 77–81
  necessity and, 140

G

Games, learning from, 20–22
Gaming industry, 178
Gates, Bill, 18, 22, 190
Geek Squad, 178
General Motors, 169
Generosity, waiting for others', 14,
      76
Gilmore, James, 177–178
Government. *See also*
      Organizations
  creation of, 155
  self-management and, 38
  smaller, 190
Granite Rock Co., 30
Grove, Andrew, 8, 156, 160

H

Habits
    decisions made by, 94
    establishing positive and elimi-
        nating negative, 115, 153–154
Hard Rock Cafe, 177, 178
Hard work. See Industry/industri-
    ousness
Hayek, Friedrich, 58, 96
Head, Howard, 20
Hobbes, Thomas, 155
Honesty
    Benjamin Franklin's view of,
        111, 113–114
    as business strategy, 93, 111,
        113–114
*How to Win Friends and Influence
    People* (Carnegie), 56
Humility, 52–53, 63, 107

I

IBM, 57
Ignorance, prison of, 11–12
Impossible, doing the, 135–143
Incentives. *See* Rewards
Industry/industriousness
    busywork vs., 76–77
    doing the impossible through,
        137
    frugality and, 70–71
    leisure vs., 82
    luck vs., 73
    modern examples of, 71–75
Influence
    highbrow vs. lowbrow, 62–64
    of peers, 94
    Socratic method and, 52
    tactics for, 60–62
Integrity, 102
Intel, 8, 109, 156
Interests
    complementary, 139–141

    shared, 52, 55
International Harvester, 162
Internet safeguard services, 143
Interviewing, behavior-based,
    41–42
Inventory control, 80
Investing, 90

J

Jefferson, Thomas, 155
Jesus, 107
Jobs, Steve, 77
Job satisfaction, 68–70, 122
Joe, Montana, 27
Jones, Arthur, 20
Junto
    Benjamin Franklin's, 23–25, 29
    modern-day, 25–27
Justice, 127
Just-in-time inventory control, 80

K

Keimer, Samuel, 43–44, 150, 186
Kelleher, Herb, 81, 171
Keller, Helen, 138–139
Kindt, John, 130

L

Landrum, Gene, 18–20, 22
Latent abilities, 138
Lawrence, D.H., 63, 110–111,
    112–113, 114–116
Lear, William, 20
Learning, lifelong
    from board games and sports,
        20–22
    of business leaders, 18–20
    companies promoting, 28–30
    discourse and, 19
    Junto and, 23–27
    meditation and, 19
    reading and, 18–20

Legacies
    Benjamin Franklin's, xviii–xx,
        188, 190
    importance of, 188
    philanthropy, 188–190
    reputation vs., 188
Leisure, 82
Leviathan (Hobbes), 155
Lies, separating truth from, 29
Locke, Edwin, 69–70
Lowenstein, Roger, xx
Luck, 14, 73, 152
Luxury, 82

M

Management. *See also* Self-manage-
    ment
    of details, 171–174
    employee motivation models,
        121–124
    force-centered vs. reasonable,
        91
    of others, 33–35
    Spartan-style, 80–81
    your example and, 34–35
Marketplace
    customer segmentation of, 160
    managing your reputation in,
        185–186
Martin, Steve, 104
Marx, Karl, 137–138
Mary Kay Cosmetics, 7–8
McCormick, Cyrus, xv
Media management, 183–184
Meditation, 19
Mellon, Thomas, xix
Microsoft, 57
Milken, Michael, 186
Mistakes, common, 13–14
Monaghan, Tom, 20
Monster.com, 141
Montana, Joe, 27

Moore, Gordon, 8, 156
Moral dilemmas. *See* Values
Morita, Akio, 20
Munger, Charles, xx

N
Nautilus Co., 20
Necessity, dangers of, 140
Networking, 72
Noyce, Bob, 8, 156
Nucor Steel, 39–41

O
Obsolescence, overcoming, 17–18
Operant conditioning, 128
Organizations
    becoming dysfunctional,
        156–157
    changes to, 157–158
    force-centered vs. reasonable,
        91
    promoting self-education,
        28–30
    reason for existence of, 155–156
Ownership, 130–131

P
Pardon, 50
Partnerships, 174–175, 177
Passion, decisions made by, 92–94
Peers, influence of, 94
The Pennsylvania Gazette, 183
People Express Airlines, 28, 39, 63
Pepsi, 59
Performance
    link between effort and, 124
    link between reward and,
        124–126
Peters, Tom, 73
Philanthropy, 188–190
Phillips, Donald, xxiii
Pine, Joseph, 177–178
Planet Hollywood, 177

Poor Richard's Almanac, 36, 64, 111, 184
Porras, Jerry, 110
Porter, Michael, 57
Presentations, 86–87
Pricing strategies, 100
Pride, 63
Prime Time Shuttle, 130–131
Prisons, types of, 10–13
Procrastination, 173
Productivity, 69–70, 122
Profiles of Genius (Landrum), 18–20
Promises, relying on, 76
Property, private, 131
The Protestant Work Ethic and the Spirit of Capitalism (Weber), xviii
Punishments, 126, 128–129

Q
Quakers, 134, 136, 143

R
Rainforest Cafe, 178
Read, Deborah, xvii
Reading
    Benjamin Franklin's, 16, 20, 21
    importance of, 18–20, 21
Reason
    caution about, 94–96
    force vs., 91
    investing and, 90
    using, in presentations, 86–87
Reengineering, 150–153
Reputation
    debt repayment and, 186–188
    importance of, 181–183
    legacy vs., 188–191
    managing, in the marketplace, 185–186
    managing, in the media, 183–184

Response, speed of, 74
Rewards
    Benjamin Franklin's method of, 120–121
    for effort, 125
    justice and, 127
    link between employee values and, 126
    link between performance and, 124–126
    punishments vs., 126, 128–129
    risk-taking and, 127
Risk-taking, 127
Rockefeller, John D., 5–6, 181–183, 184, 188–189, 191

S
Segment zero phenomenon, 160
Self-deception, 29
Self-education. See Learning, life-long
Self-help, 36
Self-improvement, 36
Self-interest, 121–124
Self-management
    assessment of, 41–42
    dangers of, 42–44
    by employees, 39–42
    government and, 38
    importance of, 35–36
Self Management Assessment Questionnaire, 41, 42
Self Reliance Inventory, 41
ServiceMaster, 9
The Seven Habits of Highly Effective People (Covey), xix
Skinner, B.F., 128–129
Sloan, Alfred P., Jr., 169
Smith, Adam, 26, 121, 155
Social problems, 142–143, 191
Socrates, 52, 53, 55, 107
Socratic method, 51–56

Sony, 20
Southwest Airlines, 81, 157, 171
Spartan-style management, 80–81
Sports
    Benjamin Franklin's participa-
        tion in, 36–38
    extreme, 38–39
    traditional competitive, 22, 37,
        38, 47–48
Springfield Remanufacturing,
    161–163
Stack, Jack, 162
Standard Oil Co., 5, 6, 182
Standard Parking, 178
Status quo, accepting, 13
Steel industry, 39–41
Success, being moderate in, 12
Sullivan, Anne, 138–139
Swimming, 36–38

T

Tarbell, Ida, 182
Technologies
    new, 78
    using appropriate, 77–78
Tennet, Gilbert, 60–61
Tit-for-Tat, 49

Tracy, Detective Dick, 60
Trash, improving upon, 9
Turner, Ted, 18, 20, 22, 190
Twain, Mark, 63

V

Value-added activities, 80
Values
    of companies, 109
    creating your own, 101–104
    identifying and clarifying,
        104–105
    turning into behavioral goals,
        107–108
von Mises, Ludwig, 58
"Vuja daze," 74–75

W

Wade, Marion, 9
Wal-Mart, 62, 71, 81
Walt Disney Co., 6–7, 115, 159,
    177, 178
Walton, Sam, 62, 64, 70–71, 81
The Wealth of Nations (Smith), 26,
    121, 155
Weber, Max, xviii

About Entrepreneur

Entrepreneur Media Inc., founded in 1973, is the nation's leading authority on small and entrepreneurial businesses.

Anchored by *Entrepreneur* magazine, which is read by more than 2 million people monthly, Entrepreneur Media boasts a stable of magazines, including *Entrepreneur's Business Start-ups, Entrepreneur International, Entrepreneur's Be Your Own Boss, Entrepreneur's Home Office* e-zine, and *Entrepreneur Mexico.*

But Entrepreneur Media is more than just magazines. Entrepreneur.com is the world's largest Web site devoted to small business and features smallbizsearch.com, a search engine targeting small-business topics. Entrepreneur Media also sponsors a series of small-business expos across the country and launched a nationwide seminar series in 2000.

Entrepreneur Press, started in 1998, publishes books to inspire and inform readers. For information about a customized version of this book, contact Jere L. Calmes at (949) 261-2325 x135 or e-mail him at jcalmes@entrepreneur.com.

Current titles from Entrepreneur Press

Business Plans Made Easy:
It's Not as Hard as You Think

Financial Fitness in 45 Days:
The Complete Guide to Shaping Up Your Finances

Gen E: Generation Entrepreneur Is Rewriting the Rules of
Entrepreneurship—And You Can, Too!

Get Smart: 365 Tips
to Boost Your Entrepreneurial IQ

Knock-Out Marketing: Powerful Strategies
to Punch Up Your Sales

Start Your Own Business:
The Only Start-Up Book You'll Ever Need

Success for Less: 100 Low-Cost Businesses
You Can Start Today

303 Marketing Tips Guaranteed
to Boost Your Business

Young Millionaires: Inspiring Stories
to Ignite Your Entrepreneurial Dreams

Where's The Money? Sure-Fire Financial Solutions
for Your Small Business

Forthcoming titles from Entrepreneur Press

Radicals & Visionaries: Entrepreneurs
Who Revolutionized the 20th Century

Creative Selling:
Unleash Your Sales Potential

How to be a Teenage Millionaire: Start Your Own Business,
Make Your Own Money and Run Your Own Life

Extreme Investor

How to Dot.Com: A Step-by-Step
Guide to E-Commerce

Extreme Entrepreneur

About The Author

Blaine McCormick, Ph.D., grew up in Lamesa, Texas, working on the family cotton farms and in the family-owned oil-and-gas distribution business. After graduating from college, he worked in Dallas and Plano for Arco as a human resources management professional. He left corporate life in 1992 to become a college professor.

After receiving his doctorate in management from Texas A&M University, he has held faculty appointments at both Pepperdine University in Los Angeles and at Baylor University in Waco, Texas. He is currently a management professor at the Hankamer School of Business at Baylor University where he teaches negotiation and conflict resolution, principles of management, and strategy and policy. He has used *The Autobiography of Benjamin Franklin* as required reading in his Introduction to Management classes for the past three years.

Blaine McCormick is also the author of *At Work With Thomas Edison: 10 Business Lessons From America's Greatest Innovator*. He is available to conduct management seminars and workshops. You can contact him at Baylor University at (254) 710-2261 or at Blaine_McCormick@baylor.edu.

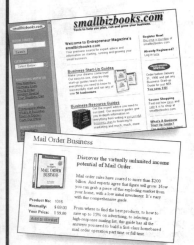

FREE ADVICE

When was the last time you got **free** advice that was worth something?

free issue!

Entrepreneur Magazine, the leading small business authority, is loaded with free advice—advice that could be worth millions to you. Every issue gives you detailed, practical knowledge on how to start a business and run it successfully. Entrepreneur is the perfect resource to keep small business owners up-to-date, on track, and growing their business.

BREAK OUT

Business Start-Ups helps you **break** out of the 9–5 life!

free issue!

Do you want to get out of the 9–5 routine and take control of your life? Business Start-Ups shows you the franchise and business opportunities that will give you the future you dream of. Every issue answers your questions, highlights hot trends, spotlights new ideas, and provides the inspiration and real-life information you need to succeed.

MILLION DOLLAR SECRETS

free issue!

Exercise your right to make it big.
Get into the small business authority—
now at 80% off the newsstand price!

Yes! Start my one year subscription and bill me for just $9.99. I get a full year of Entrepreneur and save 80% off the newsstand rate. If I choose not to subscribe, the free issue is mine to keep.

Name ☐ Mr. ☐ Mrs. _____
(please print)

Address _____

City_____ State _____ Zip_____

☐ BILL ME   ☐ PAYMENT ENCLOSED

Guaranteed. Or your money back. Every subscription to Entrepreneur comes with a 100% satisfaction guarantee: your money back whenever you like, for whatever reason, on all unmailed issues! Offer good in U.S. and possessions only. Please allow 4–6 weeks for mailing of first issue. Canadian and foreign: $39.97. U.S. funds only.

5G9J9

Mail this coupon to **Entrepreneur** MAGAZINE P.O. Box 50368, Boulder, CO 80321-0368

OPPORTUNITY KNOCKS!!!

save 72%!

free issue!

Please enter my subscription to Business Start-Ups for one year. I will receive 12 issues for only $9.99. That's a savings of 72% off the newsstand price. The free issue is mine to keep, even if I choose not to subscribe.

Name ☐ Mr. ☐ Mrs. _____
(please print)

Address _____

City_____ State _____ Zip_____

☐ BILL ME

☐ PAYMENT ENCLOSED

Mail this coupon to

Entrepreneur's Business Start·Ups

P.O. Box 50347
Boulder, CO 80321-0347

Guaranteed. Or your money back. Every subscription to Business Start-Ups comes with a 100% satisfaction guarantee: your money back whenever you like, for whatever reason, on all unmailed issues! Offer good in U.S. and possessions only. Please allow 4–6 weeks for mailing of first issue. Canadian and foreign: $34.97. U.S. funds only.

5HBK2